FOOD fight!

WITHDRAWN

A Mouthwatering History of
WHO Ate WHAT and
WHY Through the Ages

By Tanya Steel

With 30 Recipes

NATIONAL GEOGRAPHIC
WASHINGTON, D.C.

Dedication

I dedicate this book to YOU, dear reader, and to all the millions of other children around the world, to better inspire you and them to be the greatest, happiest, healthiest, and smartest people ever. I also dedicate this to my sons, William and Sanger Steel, for whom my husband and I do everything (and we mean that literally and figuratively) and who will always be the light of our lives and souls. Finally, to my husband of more than two decades, Bob Steel, who is the sweetest and kindest person I know.

Contents

I can't wait to dig in!

Introduction

Food. It nourishes you. It gives you energy. It keeps you alive. But it also tells a story and can be a direct connection to the ancient past. When you swirl that broccoli tree through a creamy bowl of hummus, you're doing more than eating a delicious and healthy snack. You're eating a food that Egypt's Queen Cleopatra lapped up more than 2,000 years ago, a dip that traveled across countries and centuries to become a favorite from the Middle East to the United States. Food history is a window into the lives of our collective ancestors. And you thought you were just grabbing a snack?

One thing's for sure: When hairy, short humans started pulling greens from the earth, berries off trees, and grapes from a vine, food became integral not just to their daily survival but to their happiness. More important, eating real, nutrient-rich food provided energy for our species' powerful brains. And those big brains have been responsible for the history of the world—all of the amazing breakthroughs and inventions, all of the developments, and, yes, many of the bad choices, too.

Human history, from the discovery of fire all the way up to what happened yesterday, has always been powered by food.

And once you get a taste of the history of food (get it?), you'll be hungry to know more. Want to know how animal stomachs were once used? Or what was served with 10,000 biscuits at a rockin' party in 1200 B.C.? How about a surprising use for sheep poop? After you've learned about the history, you can taste it by using the recipes in each chapter that are inspired by, or adapted from, the eras in which they appear. (Be sure to upload photos of your version of the dishes at kidfoodfight.com— plus find more recipes to cook up— or on Instagram with #natgeofoodfight.)

Remember: knowledge + determination + good health = the best you YOU can be. So read on and start cooking up some big dreams!

P.S. A portion of the author's proceeds from this book will go to national and international children's charities, so thank you for helping children in the United States and around the world!

Tanya Steel

Safety Tips

We know you're excited to get cooking, but before you get started, here are some safety tips we recommend you follow:

a ALWAYS have adult supervision when cooking.

b Always wash your hands.

c Keep your kitchen and food surfaces clean.

d Be sure to wash fruits and vegetables well before using.

e Keep raw foods away from cooked foods.

f Keep seafood, eggs, raw meat, and poultry separate from other foods.

g Wear short sleeves or roll up shirt sleeves while cooking to avoid getting burned.

h Clip hair up or tie it back to avoid getting food in it.

i Read the entire recipe and follow the directions.

j Have an adult help when using the stove, oven, other electrical appliances, and knives.

k Have an adult show you the correct way to use the stove, oven, kitchen appliances, and knives.

l Keep your fingers away from the sharp edges of knives and always cut away from yourself when using a knife.

m Be careful around hot surfaces and objects such as hot stoves, ovens, and dishes.

n Use oven mitts/gloves when handling hot pots, pans, and other objects.

o Make sure that pot and pan handles are turned toward the back of the stove when cooking.

p Clean up any food spills right away, especially if the spill is on the floor.

Let's cook up a storm!

The Prehistoric Era:
Cave Kids, Catching Dinner, and Camp Cookouts

A BITE-SIZE history

> "I'm hungry!" This basic thought—one we all experience every day—likely made us the exceptional species that we are today.

Finding something good to eat is probably what drove the first upright species, *Australopithecus afarensis,* to wander Earth about four million years ago. A million years later, during the Paleolithic era, or Stone Age, more human-like species, such as the Neanderthals, came and went, searching for food. After all, there weren't exactly restaurants on every block.

Humans evolved from *Homo habilis,* our first ancestors, in what is now Africa from around 2.4 million years ago until 1.5 million years ago. They had larger brains than those that had come before them (although their brains were half the size of ours today). *Homo habilis* didn't have a language and looked different from people today. Their average height was only four feet; they had more hair, longer arms, shorter legs, and a bowlegged walk. They appeared more ape than human and probably all could have used a good shampoo, conditioner, and comb out!

Eventually, about a million years ago, *Homo erectus* (a human species that came after *habilis*) discovered how to control the high-tech tool known as fire. And life got a whole lot easier. Now food could be cooked and *Homo erectus* could keep warm.

About 250,000 years ago, *Homo sapiens* (that's us) appeared on the scene in Africa. Some of them packed up their stone tools and furry clothes about 100,000 years later and hit the road for colder areas in what are now Europe and Asia. Some made it as far north as present-day Siberia above the Arctic Circle and as far south as Australia. Others may have even crossed the land bridge that once linked what are now Russia and Alaska.

Land and ice caps 12,000 years ago. Antarctica is not shown.

HOMO ERECTUS PLAYS WITH FIRE.

And that's without GPS! As groups scattered across the globe, customs, early languages, and foods began to be shared.

Fast-forward to the Neolithic era, from 15,000 to 2000 B.C. During this time, someone had a brilliant idea: If animals were kept in pens, no one would have to chase down dinner, literally. Technology continued to develop; metal tools were used; homes were built out of mud, reeds, and timber; and permanent villages appeared. Next, *Homo sapiens* figured out that by planting seeds they could grow specific foods, like wheat, barley, corn, and rice. This gave them the freedom to choose what they wanted to eat and when, and it enabled them to store food for winter and hard times.

This steadier food source helped the population flourish. About 8,000 years ago, after the glaciers had retreated and the Ice Age ended, Earth's population soared from two million—roughly the population of Nebraska today—to more than five million, about the population of Colorado now. People lived longer and now typically reached "old age" in their 40s—a nice change from the shorter life spans earlier hunters had faced. (Taking down a woolly mammoth with just a pointed stick was a dangerous job, after all.)

Once people started settling in villages, the practice of burying their dead began. The burials were either a mourning ritual or a way to prevent the dead from being scavenged by animals or birds. Around 50,000 years ago or so, spiritual beliefs began to develop. Maybe *Homo sapiens* began to realize the universe went beyond their local village?

While there is no evidence of governments or rulers from this time period, there's plenty of proof of an artistic culture. Without a written language, people expressed themselves through pictures and created the world's first art. Drawings of hands and animals have been discovered in caves and on rocks in France, Spain, Italy, Siberia, Africa, and Australia. Music also existed, with rocks and animal-skin-topped drums to keep the beat, and pipe instruments—made with hollowed-out bones that resembled the recorder many students play in school today—provided the tune.

By the end of the Neolithic era, needle and thread, clothes, and even the wheel had been invented. Humans were beginning to look, sound, live, and act more like we do today. But what and how did they eat?

> **Man still bears in his bodily frame the indelible stamp of his lowly origin.**
> Scientist Charles Darwin

Because there is evidence that tools made of specific materials were used at certain times, scientists sometimes divide the prehistoric era into three general eras:

The Stone Age
(about 2.5 million years ago to 3300 B.C.)

The Bronze Age
(about 3200 B.C. to 1300 B.C.)

The Iron Age
(about 1200 B.C. to 600 B.C.)

GATHERING CORN AND SQUASH

A DAY in the Life: Africa, 10,000 B.C.

Rise and shine! Early human children likely woke at dawn, some under fur blankets in a dark cave or a hut constructed from mud bricks or logs and tree branches. Others slept outside next to a gurgling stream.

Breakfast time! Every meal was a campfire cookout. But first, the food had to be gathered, which might mean chasing it, picking it from bushes, or plucking it out of the earth or from a tree. The food could then be roasted or boiled over the fire.

Chore time! It's likely that picking berries, fruits, nuts, veggies, and plants near the group's site would fill a kid's day. Part of the day might also have been spent building or tending an oven: Rocks were laid on top of a makeshift hole in the ground, a fire was started inside, and more rocks were placed on top of that. Butchered meat went on top of the hot rocks and then was covered with plants or vegetables and more rocks or earth. Sometimes the meat took a few days to cook, and everyone would wait, sleeping by the oven until it was ready.

Downtime! When everyone finished gathering food for the day, kids could hang with friends, maybe throwing animal bones or decorating cave walls with paints made from minerals or charcoal. Then as night fell, they'd lie down with their clan (a group of connected families), listening to nature's music—the grunts, calls, and snorts of the animals all around—as they peeked out, staring at nature's masterpiece, the Milky Way, for a long night's sleep before doing it all over again the next day.

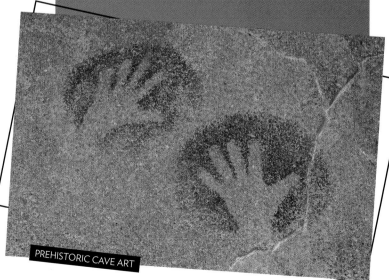
PREHISTORIC CAVE ART

Spicing Things Up!

Ever think you were so hungry you could eat a mastodon? Some prehistoric families did just that. What people ate completely depended upon where they wandered and settled. Some consumed mostly fruits and veggies, while others were more carnivorous, or meat-eating.

How did they know if something was safe to eat? Trial and error. If someone saw an animal or human get sick after eating a mushroom or drinking water from a certain spot, chances are they'd avoid that place or item and warn others from it, too.

To preserve food, some clans in colder regions used rocks to weigh down dead animals to store them in ponds, streams, and lakes when they knew the water would freeze. It was an early version of a frozen dinner!

Table matters!

Prehistoric peeps didn't sit at tables or use utensils to eat, and the idea of a napkin was thousands of years away, but there were customs and rules.

Generally, the hunters and older men ate first and had the most, followed by the women and children. The good old ground, with its dirt, grass, snow, leaves, and rocks, served as both table and chairs. Greasy fingers and faces were wiped with leaves or on cave walls or rocks, or dipped in puddles, streams, or other water.

Common foods eaten at the time:

- Birds
- Buffalo
- Rhinoceroses
- Mastodons
- Woolly mammoths
- Bears
- Seals
- Deer
- Reindeer
- Catfish
- Salmon
- Oysters
- Chickpeas
- Wheat
- Rye
- Insects
- Fruits
- Nuts
- Vegetables

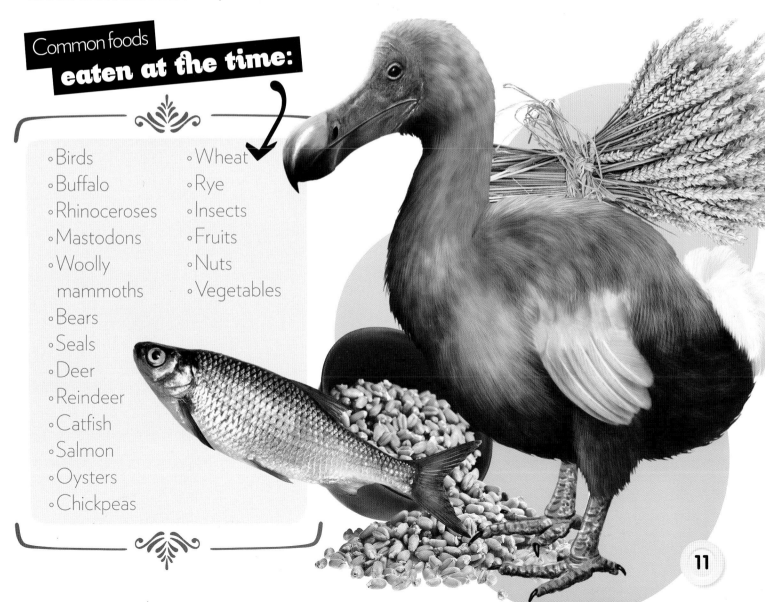

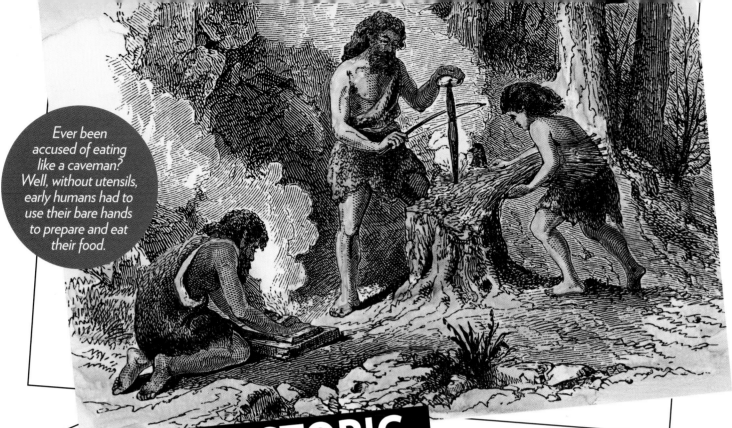

Ever been accused of eating like a caveman? Well, without utensils, early humans had to use their bare hands to prepare and eat their food.

PREHISTORIC
Kitchen Tools

STONE, WOOD, BONE, PLANTS, AND SHELLS WERE USED TO CREATE ALMOST EVERY TOOL INVENTED IN THE PALEOLITHIC AND NEOLITHIC ERAS. SOME OF THESE INCLUDED:

Spears, Harpoons, Bows, and Arrows

Sharp chiseled stones or long pointed sticks could wound or kill fish and animals.

Nets

Made of plant fibers, these enabled clans to catch more than one fish at a time.

Stone Axes

Used for everything from cutting down trees to butchering a woolly mammoth.

Stone Plow

When attached to an ox, it turned the earth and made crop tending easier.

Wheel

Probably the most important tool after fire, the wheel was invented around 3500 B.C., and the reason is surprising—for potters to make clay pots. Several hundred years later, someone had an *aha!* moment and attached a wheel to a wagon to haul heavy things.

Grinding Wheel

This large stone wheel smashed plants and seeds and turned them into grains and flours.

Mortar and Pestle

This shallow stone bowl (the mortar) and heavy mini-baseball-bat-like club (the pestle) was invented in 35,000 B.C. for pulverizing and combining tough or hard ingredients.

Cooking Equipment

During the Paleolithic era, large oyster or clam shells and hollowed-out animal stomachs and stone vessels were used to cook foods. These were mostly replaced by clay pots in the Neolithic era.

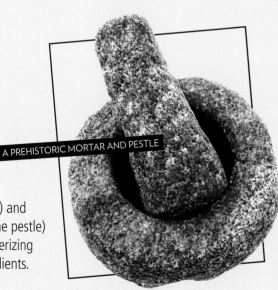

A PREHISTORIC MORTAR AND PESTLE

YUCKY HABITS OF YORE

Early humans ate what was available, including insects! Mmm ... cicadas?

Humans used animal stomachs to carry, store, and cook food. A prehistoric backpack!

MENUS OF THE Rich & Famished

There is no evidence of what prehistoric people ate on special occasions. Perhaps they had roasted woolly mammoth served with boiled green onions, pulverized sesame seeds, and egret soup? Ummm ... yum?

By the Numbers

5 BILLION: Number of species on Earth in the prehistoric era.

10 TO 14 MILLION: Number of species on Earth in the early 21st century.

5,500 YEARS: Age of the oldest bread ever found.

4,000 YEARS: Age of the oldest noodles ever found.

5,000 YEARS: Age of the oldest butter ever found.

At some point in the prehistoric era, Neanderthal and *Homo sapiens* crossed gene pools. That means today some humans carry a tiny bit of Neanderthal genes! So when someone says, "Stop acting like a Neanderthal," you can say, "I'm just doing what's natural ..."

Eat THIS

ROAST MASTODON ON A STICK

Cooking meat on a stick is as old as human-kind. Prehistoric people were not picky about what types of meat they ate, from enormous mastodons to rhinos to pigeons. And they used any reed, bamboo, or stick they could hold over an open fire. Since mastodons have been extinct for 10,000 years, it's OK to substitute any available meat, from sirloin to chicken.

Makes 4 Servings

1 pound (456 g) beef, fat trimmed, cut into about 1-inch chunks

1 medium onion, peeled and coarsely chopped

1 red bell pepper, seeds removed, cut into 1 x 1–inch strips

16 cherry tomatoes

8 long wooden skewers, soaked in water for 1 hour, or stainless steel skewers

1/4 cup (60 ml) olive oil

Pinch of salt and pepper and any other seasonings you like

1   Ask an adult to preheat the grill or broiler to medium. Meanwhile, on each skewer, put one piece of beef, one piece of onion, and one bell pepper strip, and repeat with remaining ingredients and skewers so each skewer has several pieces of beef, onion, and pepper. Place a tomato on either end of each skewer. Brush the olive oil on the skewered ingredients with a pastry brush or drizzle it over with a spoon.

2   Ask an adult to place the meat on the grill and cook, turning after 5 minutes. Cook about 3 minutes more, or until cooked through and brown and crispy. Take the food off the skewer with a fork, season to taste, and then put down your prehistoric club and put on your furry bib before you eat it.

Hammond, 14, recommends seasoning the meat with paprika or other spices for added flavor.

CAVE KID TRAIL MIX

Before diners, fast-food chains, and food trucks, there was the trail. When kids walked from place to place, they gathered food as they went. Nuts, berries, and fruits were all there for the taking. This recipe contains many ingredients a prehistoric man, woman, or child might have eaten.

Makes 4 Servings

1 cup (125 g) unsalted shelled pecans

1 cup (140 g) unsalted shelled almonds

1 cup (125 g) unsalted shelled walnuts

2 teaspoons (10 ml) melted coconut oil or olive oil

1 tablespoon (15 ml) honey

1/2 cup (65 g) raw pumpkin seeds

1/2 cup (70 g) sunflower seeds

1/2 teaspoon (2.5 g) salt

1/2 cup (75 g) raisins or dried cranberries

1   Ask an adult to preheat the oven to 375°F/190°C. Spread the pecans, almonds, and walnuts on a large shallow baking sheet, drizzle with 1 teaspoon oil and the honey, and stir. Ask an adult to place in the oven to roast for 7 minutes, or until fragrant and lightly toasted. Ask an adult to remove from the oven.

2   While the nuts are roasting, ask an adult to warm the remaining teaspoon of oil in a medium skillet over low heat. Add the pumpkin and sunflower seeds. Cook, shaking the pan, until the seeds are fragrant, 3 to 5 minutes. Remove from the heat.

3   Transfer to a medium bowl and add the salt. When the nuts are ready and have cooled, add to the seeds and toss. Add the raisins or cranberries; toss again and let cool. Store in a covered glass jar or plastic container.

66 We tried it with cranberries, which gave it a sweet and tangy flavor. Loved this mix! 99 Laura, 15

POP CORNY quiz

1

When do scientists think humans discovered fire?

A. 1 million years ago
B. 10 million years ago
C. 100,000 years ago
D. The day you were born
E. Yesterday

3

What were harpoons originally used for?

A. To throw in competitions
B. To use as sticks to make a fort
C. To kill fish and animals
D. As very large toothpicks
E. As kebab skewers

2

What didn't the prehistoric human invent?

A. Plow
B. Wheel
C. Fur coat
D. iPad
E. Needle and thread

4

How did prehistoric people know what was safe to eat?

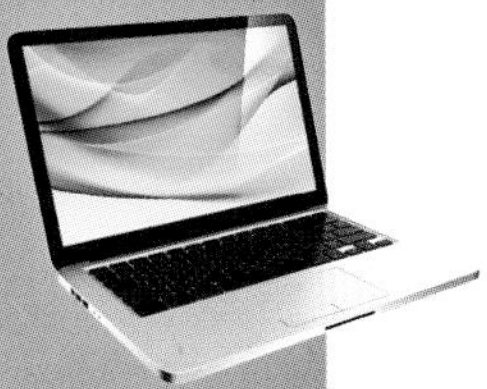

A. Trial and error.
B. They looked it up on the Internet.
C. They read it in a book.
D. They asked the animals and plants.
E. They asked the aliens.

5

What wasn't used as a cooking pot or vessel?

A. Clam shell
B. Oyster shell
C. Stone pot
D. Animal stomach
E. Bird beak

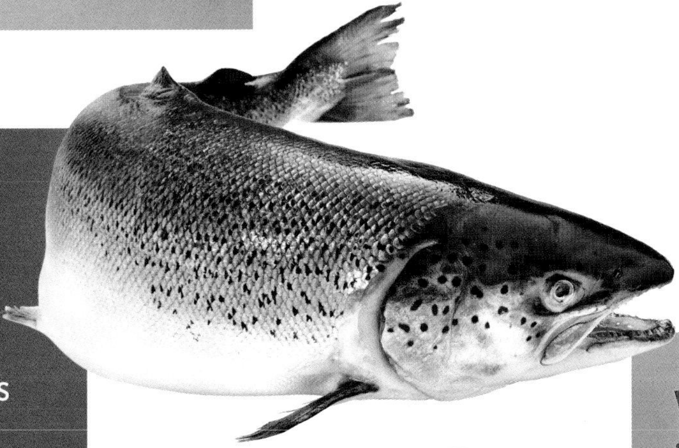

6

Which were common prehistoric foods?

A. Nuts and berries
B. Fish
C. Mastodons
D. Buffalo
E. All of the above

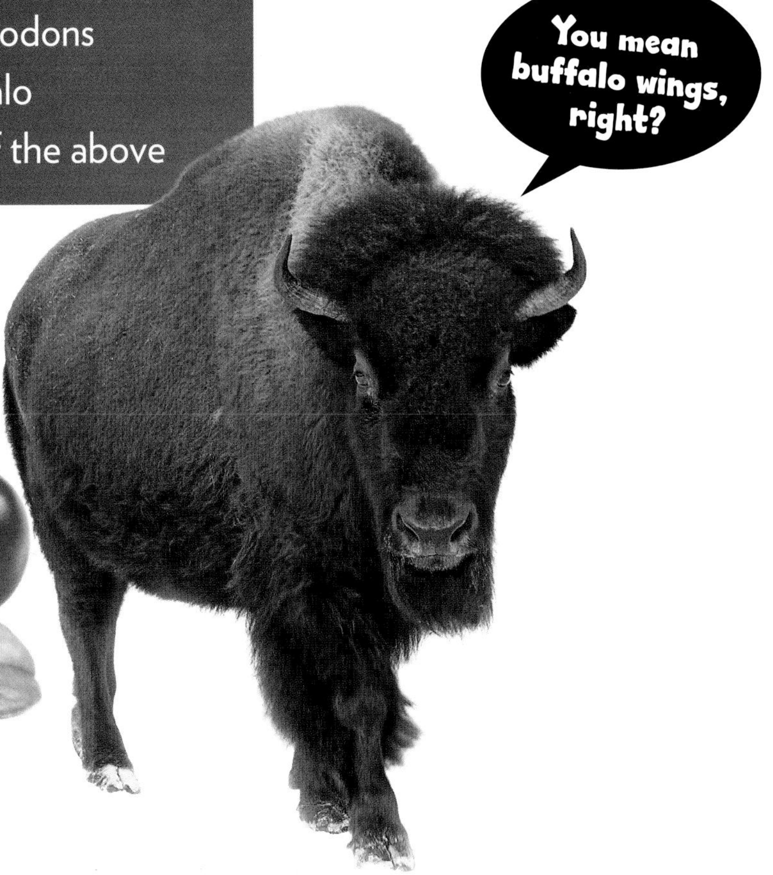

You mean buffalo wings, right?

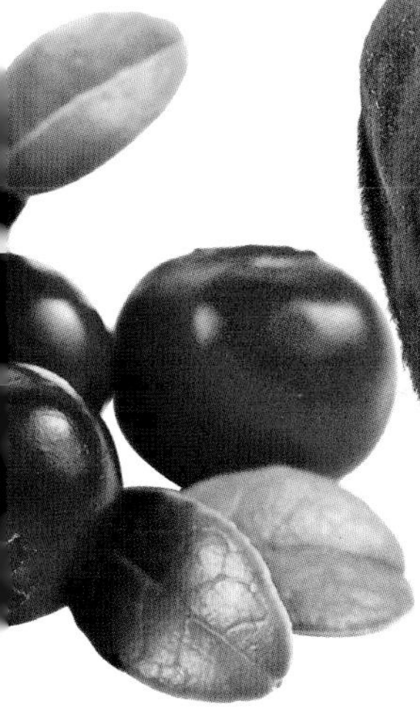

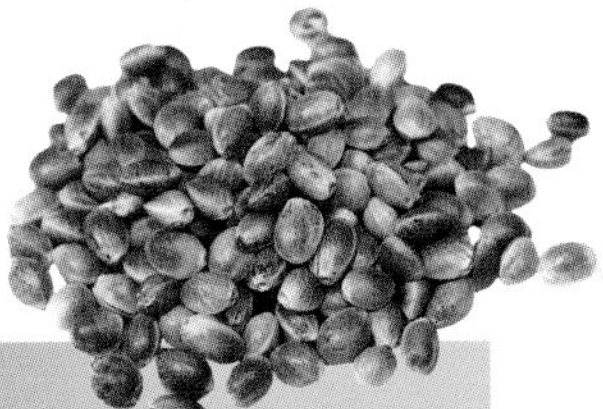

7

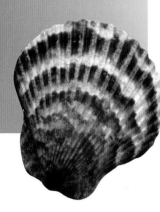

Why was planting seeds important for prehistoric people?

A. They could count on food growing.
B. They could choose what they ate.
C. They could store some food for winter.
D. They could sell their seeds online.
E. All but D.

Answers: 1. A; 2. D; 3. C; 4. A; 5. E; 6. E; 7. E

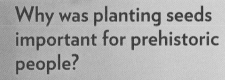

Egypt: Feasts for Mummies, Mommies, and Pharaohs

A BITE-SIZE history

Inside a dark cave lay a linen-wrapped mummy, a boy king who lived more than 3,000 years ago. Sitting beside him were more than a hundred baskets containing melons, grapes, wheat, barley, and honey. Who was this mysterious king and why was he buried with his favorite snacks? Let's find out.

While humans have lived in the sandy area around what is now Egypt since about 40,000 B.C., Egypt was officially united about 3150 B.C. by King Menes (also known as Narmer). As Egypt's first king, he brought together several neighboring settlements and then built a city, Memphis, south of the Nile River and made it the capital. (The American city Memphis, Tennessee, was named after the original one in Egypt!)

The pharaohs (another word for ruler) that followed King Menes created the world's first bureaucracy, a government with many departments each responsible for specific duties, similar to the United States government today. Egypt had rich aristocrats who ruled over their local regions as governors, as well as a small middle class made up of merchants, craftsmen, and government workers. But the majority of the population were peasant farmers who grew food or flax, a plant that was turned into linen to make clothes.

Around 2550 B.C., the pharaoh Khufu decided to build what remains one of the world's most extraordinary achievements—the Great Pyramids, which still exist in and around Giza, Egypt, more than 4,500 years later! Created as royal burial chambers, these enormous triangular buildings took hundreds of thousands of workers many decades to construct. To build them, more than two million two-ton (1.8-t) granite and limestone blocks were transported to Giza via rafts on the Nile. The royals entombed in the pyramids were mummified

after death to preserve their bodies for the afterlife they believed in. Mummification was a process in which a body was hollowed out, stuffed with linens and spices, and then wrapped in more linen. The royals were buried with many of their possessions and favorite foods to help keep them happy and well fed in the afterlife.

As the pyramids were being built, a system of writing called hieroglyphics developed. It used more than 3,100 symbols and pictures—examples can be seen today on the Rosetta Stone at the British Museum in London, England— and became the original form of written communication. Scribes or clerks copied documents on sheets of papyrus (paper made from the papyrus plant) or on walls using reed pens and plant ink, or they chiseled pictures into stone. They even wrote down detailed directions for how to perform brain surgery!

Around 2055 B.C., a struggle between Egypt's powerful regional governors, along with crop failures and economic problems due to the expense of building the pyramids, caused a series of small civil wars. The result was the unification of all of Egypt's regions under just one king. Then in 1700 B.C., foreign invaders from western Asia known as the Hyksos used horse-drawn chariots and bronze weapons—military technology never before seen in Egypt—to take over. Egyptians took back control in the 1500s B.C., and the pharaohs went on to expand their empire into the Middle East and farther into Africa.

Cairo
Giza
Memphis
Nile
EGYPT
Nile
Present-day boundaries are shown.

A RELIC FROM ABOUT 3100 B.C. CELEBRATING KING MENES

One of Egypt's pharaohs was a woman named Hatshepsut who reigned from 1478 to 1458 B.C. with her stepson Thutmose III. Women in Egypt had more rights than those in many future civilizations—they could inherit property, get a divorce, and have a job.

But perhaps most famous of all was the pharaoh Tutankhamun, also known as King Tut. He was only nine years old when he began to rule (1332 to about 1323 B.C.), which is why he was also called "the Boy King." Tut reigned until he died at the age of 18 or 19. A solid gold death mask found in his tomb revealed what he looked like.

Egypt's last pharaoh was the beautiful Cleopatra VII, who became queen at 18 and ruled until she died at 39. But her reign wasn't easy or peaceful. She got help from Rome's Julius Caesar (see page 40), and after Caesar's death, she joined forces with Rome's general Mark Antony against Caesar's heir. She lost Egypt to Rome, which brought an end to Egyptian pharaohs.

One-quarter of what you eat keeps you alive. The **other three-quarters** keeps your doctor alive.

Hieroglyphs in an Egyptian tomb about the perils of eating unhealthy food

King Tut was 5'11", which was really tall back then.

AN EGYPTIAN TOMB PAINTING

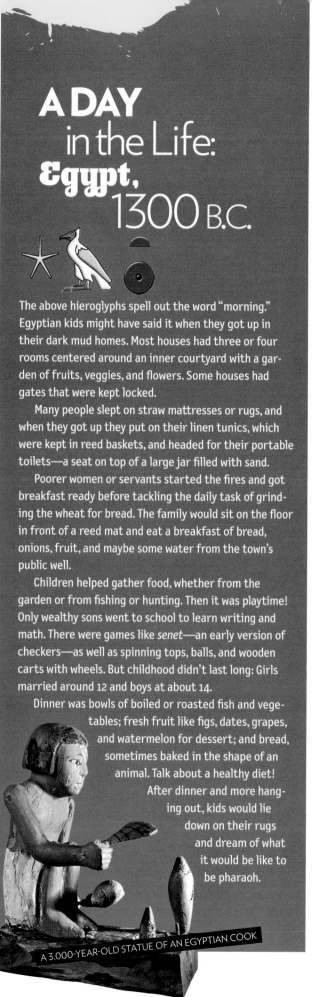

A DAY
in the Life:
Egypt, 1300 B.C.

The above hieroglyphs spell out the word "morning." Egyptian kids might have said it when they got up in their dark mud homes. Most houses had three or four rooms centered around an inner courtyard with a garden of fruits, veggies, and flowers. Some houses had gates that were kept locked.

Many people slept on straw mattresses or rugs, and when they got up they put on their linen tunics, which were kept in reed baskets, and headed for their portable toilets—a seat on top of a large jar filled with sand.

Poorer women or servants started the fires and got breakfast ready before tackling the daily task of grinding the wheat for bread. The family would sit on the floor in front of a reed mat and eat a breakfast of bread, onions, fruit, and maybe some water from the town's public well.

Children helped gather food, whether from the garden or from fishing or hunting. Then it was playtime! Only wealthy sons went to school to learn writing and math. There were games like *senet*—an early version of checkers—as well as spinning tops, balls, and wooden carts with wheels. But childhood didn't last long: Girls married around 12 and boys at about 14.

Dinner was bowls of boiled or roasted fish and vegetables; fresh fruit like figs, dates, grapes, and watermelon for dessert; and bread, sometimes baked in the shape of an animal. Talk about a healthy diet! After dinner and more hanging out, kids would lie down on their rugs and dream of what it would be like to be pharaoh.

A 3,000-YEAR-OLD STATUE OF AN EGYPTIAN COOK

Spicing Things Up!

Since Egyptians lived near or on the Nile River, they ate a lot of fish. From catfish and perch to eels and tilapia, fish was almost as plentiful as Egypt's sand. The fish was roasted, broiled, and boiled, made into fish cakes, or dried in the sun to eat weeks later.

The Nile also attracted a lot of wildlife, which men, boys, and slaves would hunt. Wild geese, ducks, pigeons, and even antelope were the usual prey. Antelope burgers, anyone?

Sweet foods were often made with dates from Egypt's most abundant tree, the date palm. These bite-size fruits were not only a go-to and to-go snack but also natural sweeteners for cakes, pastries, and stews.

Where did Egyptians bake up these sweet treats? The courtyard in most well-to-do family homes functioned as a kitchen, dining room, and playground. It included a clay oven or a fire pit where desserts and pita bread and everything from fish to fowl could be cooked. Some homes even cooked on rooftop terraces using portable grill-like devices called braziers.

Archaeologists discovered one house from the time that had not just one but three ovens! Whoever owned that home clearly cooked a lot; some think it was part of a megamansion with a large staff.

Whether they were rich or poor, many families kept sheep and goats to provide milk and wool, and most had kitchen gardens, which supplied ingredients like onions, cabbage, and melons.

Table matters!

Where people ate depended very much on whether they were noble or not. Aristocrats and royals sat on cushions around low tables, although some pharaohs sat at tables with metal lions for legs. The majority of people likely crouched around or on reed mats. Archaeologists have uncovered paintings on pottery and in tombs, showing people eating and drinking. They've also found actual Egyptian tables, which are exhibited in museums today.

Pots were made of copper and bronze; knives of stone and bronze; spoons of wood or metal. Some families did have clay plates, and the pharaohs' dishes were made of gold and silver. Everyone ate from shared ceramic bowls filled with hummus or roast fish and veggies, eagerly but politely taking turns to serve themselves with their fingers or scooping out food with bread. They rinsed their fingers in small water-filled dishes as they went.

A PAGE FROM THE ANCIENT EGYPTIAN *BOOK OF THE DEAD*

Common foods eaten in Egypt at the time:

- Geese
- Ducks
- Pelicans
- Gazelles
- Oxen
- Emmer
  (a type of wheat)
- Barley
- Chickpeas
- Cucumbers
- Lettuce
- Onions
- Garlic
- Melons
- Figs
- Carob
- Honey

Found in Thebes, these tomb wall paintings show food's importance.

EGYPTIAN
Kitchen Tools

WHILE EGYPTIAN FOOD WAS HEALTHY AND DELICIOUS, PEOPLE HAD TO WORK FOR THEIR SUPPER; MUCH OF THE DAY WAS SPENT HARVESTING, CATCHING, AND COOKING FOOD.

Fishing Equipment

Linen nets and fishing lines with hooks made from bone, wood, or shells were used to catch fish. Clay was used to weight fishing lines, and willow branches were the material for fish traps and baskets.

Irrigation System

Every summer, the Nile flooded Egypt's deserts and watered the crops, but when it didn't flood, Egyptians used an advanced bucket system to water crops.

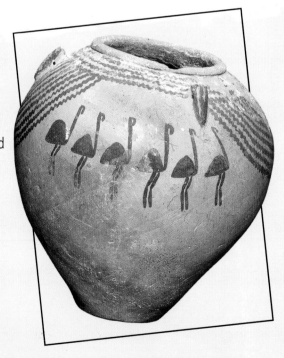

Glass

Given Egypt's desert, it's not surprising they figured out sand could be transformed into glass. Invented and perfected in Egypt, glass was used in sculptures, jewelry, elegant jars, and, oh yes, drinking glasses.

Clay Jars

Pottery was mass-produced and families kept large clay jars filled with nonperishables like lentils, barley, farro, and dried fish for when food was scarce. It was like having canned or pickled foods in a pantry today.

By studying the teeth of mummies, scientists found that Egyptian bread usually contained some desert sand or stone dust from the wheat-grinding process.

When making a lot of bread in a large container, bakers sometimes kneaded the dough with their feet. Hopefully their feet were clean!

MENUS OF THE
Rich & Famished

At his feasts, King Merneptah, who ruled from 1213 to 1203 B.C., liked to serve sliced gazelle basted in honey. That would have looked like nothing compared to this menu for a pharaoh in the 1200s B.C. that included:

10,000 biscuits

1,200 loaves of bread

1,000 bunches of oasis grapes

300 strings of figs

250 handfuls of beef innards

100 baskets of dried meat

100 heads of lettuce

70 sheep

50 jars of honeycomb

50 jars of cucumbers

40 cooked ducks

30 jars of carob seeds with carrot pulp

12 kinds of fish

HOW CINNAMON AND OTHER SPICES CHANGED THE WORLD

While Egypt was building pyramids, India started selling its spices to the world. Spices—usually made from fruit, seeds, barks, or roots—were extremely important because they flavored and preserved food and were used as medicines, incense, and air freshener. Doctors used pepper to cure everything from headaches and fevers to chest pain.

Fearless explorers traveled to India for these treasures. And so began the spice trade, which went on for thousands of years. So when you add cinnamon to a recipe, don't take it for granted!

House Manager for Beef Fat was an official job in one of Egypt's megarich homes.

By the Numbers

40: Varieties of breads and pastries available to eat in Egypt around 2000 B.C.

5,398: Number of objects discovered in King Tut's tomb—and that was after it had been robbed!

30,000: Number of people it took to build the Great Pyramid in Giza over 20 years.

A CLAY TABLET WITH CUNEIFORM WRITING

Eat THIS

HEAVENLY HUMMUS

What a dip! That's what Cleopatra might have thought about hummus. It's perfect to slather on bread; use as a dip for carrots, sugar snap peas, and broccoli; and to add to soups and stews. Chickpeas, which are a type of legume, are packed with fiber and protein, so add them whole to any soup, roast them for a snack, or smoosh them to smithereens like we do here. Consider making extra garlic oil to drizzle on top.

Makes 4 Servings

1 15-ounce (427-g) can garbanzo beans, drained and rinsed

3 tablespoons (45 g) tahini

1/4 cup (60 ml) extra-virgin olive oil

2 garlic cloves—peeled, smashed, and finely chopped

3 tablespoons (45 ml) water

2 tablespoons (30 ml) fresh lemon juice

1/2 teaspoon (2.5 g) salt

1 Working with an adult, combine beans and tahini in a food processor or blender; process until smooth.

2 Ask an adult to warm 2 tablespoons of olive oil in a sauté pan on medium heat. Add the garlic and warm for 1 minute. Add the remaining 2 tablespoons of oil.

3 Add the warm garlicky oil to the food processor with the water, lemon juice, and salt. Process until smooth, about 30 seconds more. Walk like an Egyptian (look up the song) after eating it!

" I absolutely LOVED this dish! I can't wait to make it again! It might even be one of my new favorite foods!! It was super easy to make, and I thought it was best served with baby carrots and pita chips. "

Hannah, 14

KING TUT'S NOT FISHY CAKES

People ate so much fish in Egypt they practically had gills! Little did they know how healthy it was. They sometimes turned leftover fish into cakes like these. Serve with the hummus or lentil stew (page 34), or simply top with plain Greek yogurt and parsley. Be sure to drain the turnips and fish completely so they are easier to sauté.

Makes 4 Servings

2 large turnips—ends cut off, peeled and quartered

1 large potato, peeled and sliced

1 pound (454 g) fresh or frozen wild flaky white fish (such as cod, haddock, or tilapia)

1/4 cup (60 ml) olive oil

2 tablespoons (20 g) finely chopped onion

1/2 cup (45 g) plain dried bread crumbs

1 egg

Handful (12 g) chopped fresh parsley

1 teaspoon (2.5 g) Old Bay seasoning or paprika

Salt and pepper to taste

1 lemon, cut into quarters

1 Place the turnips and potato in a large pot of water and ask an adult to bring the water to a boil. Cook for 7 minutes.

2 Add the fish to the pot and cook until the fish, turnips, and potato are soft, about 3 minutes more. Ask an adult to drain the mixture well in a colander and transfer it to a large mixing bowl. Let cool for 5 minutes.

3 Add 2 tablespoons oil, as well as onion, bread crumbs, egg, parsley, Old Bay, and salt and pepper to the bowl; mix and mash the mixture together with your hands, and then mold it into 10 medium-size patties, putting each one on a plate as you go. (Wash your hands afterward as you've touched raw egg.)

4 Ask an adult to heat 1 tablespoon of oil in a large skillet over medium-high heat. Fry half the patties on medium heat on both sides until golden brown, about 4 minutes per side. Repeat with remaining oil and patties. Drain on paper towels before serving. Squeeze lemon juice on the cakes and top with plain yogurt, fresh herbs, lentil stew, or hummus.

" I was amazed there was fish in these and even had a second cake! "
Athena, 8

POP CORNY quiz

1

What was found often in Egyptian bread?

A. Reeds
B. Stone dust and sand
C. Yeast
D. Fish heads
E. Lucky charms

3

What was a common dessert?

A. Figs
B. Dates
C. Watermelon
D. Grapes
E. All of the above

2

Why did the kings want food in their tombs?

A. To entice people to see their tombs
B. To feed their pet cats and monkeys
C. To show the gods they were very rich
D. To feed them in their afterlife
E. In case their servants needed a quick snack

Kitty tombs?! I was just looking for the litter box ...

4

What were bodies stuffed with during mummification?

A. Gold
B. Antelope bones
C. Fish cheeks
D. Linens and spices
E. Amulets

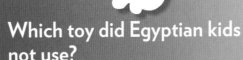

5

Which toy did Egyptian kids not use?

A. Spinning tops
B. Checkers-like game
C. Balls
D. Wooden carts on wheels
E. PlayStation 4

6

What did the Egyptians use to fish?

A. Linen
B. Willow
C. Shells
D. Clay
E. All of the above

Wealthy Egyptians brought pet monkeys or their beloved cats, which they worshipped, to parties. (Some actually prayed to a cat goddess called Bastet.)

For almost 300 years Egypt's royalty and ruling class spoke Greek instead of Egyptian because Greek was considered a more elite language.

7

What was one house manager in charge of?

A. Hosting oxen dances
B. Throwing sheep parties
C. Controlling beef fat
D. Holding dinners for ducks
E. Gathering ice skates

Greece:
Gods, Goats, and Greek Yogurt

A BITE-SIZE
history

Just across the Mediterranean Sea from Egypt, around 2500 B.C., another group of people were beginning their own equally exceptional empire.

It all started with some sheepherders known as Minoans who lived on the island of Crete in the Aegean Sea. These ambitious islanders formed a community and obeyed a king named Minos. His palace had more than 1,000 rooms, was larger than the White House and Buckingham Palace combined, and was famous for a weird new home luxury called a bathroom. His palace also had a school for children. Students learned math, science, and history—yes, even back then kids studied what people did before them!

Around 1650 B.C., the Mycenaeans, who came after the Minoans, used their powerful army to expand Greece into what is now Turkey. We know this because a man named Homer wrote about these battles in two epic poems called *The Iliad* and *The Odyssey*. By 800 B.C., Greece had grown even more and formed a new system of government called city-states, meaning places like Athens and Sparta each had their own governments and armies.

Greece managed to defeat all of its invaders, including the Persians at the Battle of Marathon in 490 B.C. As the story goes, a young Athenian named Pheidippides ran 26.2 miles (42.16 km) from Marathon to Athens to tell the Athenians of their victory over the Persians. (This is why marathons were so named and how they came to be 26.2 miles.)

The neighboring city-states of Athens and Attica decided to merge in the early fifth century B.C. to form a new type of government called a democracy—the world's first. Just like democratic countries today, citizens could vote on rules and laws. But unlike today, only free men over 18 who weren't immigrants and who had completed their military training and owned land

were considered citizens. So, little more than 10 percent of its 300,000 residents could actually vote.

While Athens was "democratic," its other city-state neighbors were not. Macedon was a dictatorship, which means one ruler has ultimate authority, and Sparta was run by not one but two kings. In Sparta, boys over the age of seven went into the military. Spartans didn't care about making money, inventing new things, or citizens' rights; they just wanted to be number one in military might. They were truly expert soldiers. In fact, when Spartan boys went into battle, their mothers' common motto was "Come home with your shield, or upon it!"

Around 431 B.C., Greece went to war ... with itself. In what is known as the Peloponnesian War, Sparta (along with Persia, Corinth, and Thebes) eventually defeated Athens in 404 B.C. and became the ruler of Greece. About a hundred years later, a new leader took charge of the coalition of Greek states, Alexander the Great. What was so great about him? He expanded Greece into an even bigger empire that included parts of what are now Iran, Iraq, Egypt, and India.

ITALY

Present-day boundaries are shown.

MACEDON

GREECE

Thebes

Corinth • • Athens

Sparta •

Aegean Sea

ATTICA

A GREEK WARRIOR

29

While Greece's empire grew, so did its amazing achievements: Artists carved huge realistic sculptures of famous people, some of which still exist today; grand buildings were decorated with elaborate columns and other architectural details that are still used today; theater lovers watched plays performed in large outdoor amphitheaters; and a sporting event called the Olympics was created.

> "With a **peaceful and healthy life** of this kind, they will no doubt reach **old age** and pass on a similar **style of life** to their offspring."
>
> Philosopher Socrates

Huge advancements were made in medicine, too. Hippocrates, now called the Father of Medicine, led the way by teaching that a good diet and exercise were critical to good health. Socrates developed the philosophy that the more one knows the better one can reason and achieve happiness.

Math and science also had major advancements during this period. Democritus believed that everything was made of microscopic and indestructible atoms, which was a radical idea. Eratosthenes was the first to accurately measure the circumference of Earth. Euclid wrote *The Elements,* which became the basis for modern geometry. Archimedes figured out how to measure an object's volume when he got into the bathtub and the water spilled out. His response? "Eureka!" (Greek for "I have found it!") And Aristarchus came up with the idea that Earth actually orbits the sun, although it took more than 1,500 years before people actually began to believe this theory!

The Greeks also invented alarm clocks, screws, water mills, odometers, automatic doors, catapults, crossbows, cement, central heating, anchors, sinks, showers, and clock towers, just to name a few things. Plus, the 12-month, 365-day calendar.

It was an advanced society, that's for sure, and shaped important parts of our lives today. So what did they eat to be so wise?

THE RUINS OF MINOS'S KNOSSOS PALACE

DETAIL OF A BANQUET SCENE IN GREECE

A DAY in the Life: Crete, 482 B.C.

"It's bright!" That might have been the first thought for children living in sunny Heraklion, Crete, who slept in hammocks near the windows in cozy white stone or mud-brick houses overlooking the sea. Homes had just a few rooms and didn't have glass windows, even though Egypt had already invented glass. Some wealthy homes had two floors, with the bedrooms upstairs as well as a special women-only room called a gynaeceum, where ladies hung out and ate.

When they got up, children would "wash" their bodies with drops of olive oil, rubbing it on like moisturizer and then scraping it and the dirt off with a spatula-like strigil. They would slip on their linen or woolen tunics that were tied at the waist and chow down on breakfast, or *akratisma.* This could be figs, olives, and a barley bread called *maza* (similar to pita bread), which was dipped in olive oil, or *tagenon,* a type of pancake drizzled with honey.

Boys went to school for reading and writing, while girls worked, weaving linens, cooking, and gardening. Before they were considered adults, around the age of 13, children spent their spare time spinning tops, playing with blown-up pig bladders (almost 2,000 years later, these became footballs, which is why they are sometimes called a pigskin), dolls, and metal hoops that were similar to Hula-Hoops today. Or they explored caves and swam in the sea.

When they needed a pick-me-up, they snacked on figs or *oxygala,* also known as yogurt—yes, Greek yogurt!—with honey. They also munched on walnuts, chickpeas, green and black olives, goat cheese, pistachios, grapes, apples, and pears.

Dinner, or *deipnon,* was served in the evening. Men and women didn't eat together at dinner, and children and slaves served food to their father. The father was literally the breadwinner—his salary often paid in bread and food instead of money, which is why he got served first.

After dinner, kids might climb back into their hammocks and look at the bright stars through their windows, thinking about the latest math or science fact they had heard that day.

Spicing Things Up!

Eating healthfully was important to Greeks; they made a direct connection between what someone ate and their health, coining the word "dietetics." The Greeks, led by Hippocrates, believed ingredients had "humors" (hot, cold, dry, and wet) and that having balanced humors was critical to good health. Children were supposed to eat dry, cold foods like aged cheeses and beans.

Even the poor and slaves had a healthy diet, eating tons of produce and seafood. They were lucky to live in a place where fresh fish was just a net's throw away, olive and citrus groves grew in people's yards, and everyone could grow their own fruits, veggies, and herbs. Still, some of the harder-to-catch oysters, sea urchins, octopuses, and eels were only eaten by the wealthy. Snails were a no-go. Goats were popular for their milk, which was made into cheese and yogurt.

Anything people couldn't grow could be bought or traded at an agora, or market. These were like farmers markets today.

Younger children went to the market, often with their father, while older kids were likely to be sent on their own to get their family's fish, produce, and daily bread. Sweets, cookware, shoes, dresses, jewelry, and cloth were also available. Many items were transported to and from the market in goatskins via donkeys.

Most homes had open-air courtyards, which also acted as kitchen, dining room, and playground. The kitchen sometimes had a wood-burning oven and a pantry area where food was kept, fish and herbs were hung to dry, and pans and jugs were stored. If the family was wealthy, tablecloths and spoons were kept in the pantry, too.

Table matters!

Mealtime was a big deal in Greece, something everyone really looked forward to. Eating was the total focus, and there was an unofficial rule that children only talked when spoken to. Some adults ate while reclining on couches.

For many families, food was placed directly onto a wooden table, which was scrubbed before and after meals. Wealthier homes used plates. Instead of napkins, most people used clothing, hands, the tablecloth, or even bread to wipe away dirt. (No trying that at dinner tonight, please!)

People usually ate with their hands, but in fancier homes they'd get a spoon for stews, soups, and yogurts. And if they had to cut meat, which was rare (get it?), a knife would be brought out. Forks were not common.

PARTY TIME: A BANQUET IN ANCIENT GREECE

Common foods eaten in Greece at the time:

- Oysters
- Sardines
- Eels
- Persimmons
- Figs
- Asparagus
- Lamb
- Goat
- Pork
- Lentils
- Chickpeas
- Honey
- Yogurt
- Nuts
- Raisins
- Cheese

Food was used in sacrifices to the gods and as a form of money: It was used to pay taxes, and three buckets of olives could buy a girl's tunic.

GREEK

Kitchen Tools

MUCH OF THE COOKING EQUIPMENT USED BY GREEKS WOULD LOOK FAMILIAR TODAY:

Mini Portable Grills

Not every home had an oven, so this was an important piece of equipment. These grills used charcoal or vine clippings as fuel. Stone, earthenware, or bronze pans were placed on top to cook fish, meat, or veggies.

Wooden Paddles

In every local square or at home, paddles were used to take bread or meat out of the oven, just like those used in pizzerias today.

Earthenware Cups

A kylix, a shallow earthenware cup, was used at fancy parties and festive occasions.

The paint used on plates was mixed with human urine to keep the paint from fading.

To heat up their ovens, Greeks used olive, oak, and beech wood, and sometimes even sheep poop.

Spartans couldn't get enough of their black broth, which was a soup thickened with animal blood.

MENUS OF THE
Rich & Famished

Wealthy Greeks were big on banquets, called symposiums. These dinner parties, which were almost always for men only, often started in the early evening; the men lay on couches with a stool next to them for their sandals. Slaves, including children, fed them bread, olives, fruit, and shellfish. Food scraps were tossed to the floor. The richer the host, the more cakes, like baklava made with phyllo dough, he offered for dessert. The parties often ended with entertainment, such as musicians or acrobats.

A warrior's feast is featured in *The Iliad*. Homer describes how goats, pigs, and sheep were chopped into pieces, skewered, salted, and roasted above the fire until crisp and served with barley bread.

At big banquets, elaborately decorated tables held the food; archaeologists found a perfectly intact table from the second century B.C. that had legs like lions' paws. Anyone who ate from it must have had a roaring good time!

THE GODS AND GODDESSES OF YUMMY FOOD

Greeks believed in many gods and goddesses, sacrificing a portion of every meal to them. A few of their faves:

Athena, Goddess of Wisdom: Athena was said to have placed her spear into the ground and turned it into the first olive tree. Greeks used olive trees for their wood, they ate its fruit, and they pressed the olives to get oil for cooking.

Hestia, Goddess of Homes: She was honored with a constantly burning hearth.

Demeter and Persephone, Goddesses of the Harvest: They were thanked for their help in growing abundant food.

Hephaestus, God of Weaponry: He was a master craftsman who invented a device that made strings of dough. Later pasta machines were based on similar concepts.

By the Numbers

2.2 POUNDS (1 KG)**:** Average annual meat consumption in first-century B.C. Greece. Today, Greeks and Americans eat about 70 pounds (32 kg) per person. The global average is about 42 pounds (19 kg) per person.

80: Percentage of the Greek diet that was made up of grains.

ABOUT 3 YEARS' WORTH: The amount of grain and olive oil most families stored in case of bad harvests.

5 MILLION: Estimated population living in Greece (which included some of Sicily and Asia Minor's coast) during the fourth century B.C. Today, 11 million people live in Greece.

40,000: Number of people who attended the first ever Olympic Games in 776 B.C.

Wealthy Greeks lit their homes with lamps that burned wicks doused in olive oil.

Eat THIS

LENTIL STEW FOR JUNIOR OLYMPIADS

Lentils were a big part of people's diets in ancient times, and we still love them, especially because we know how healthy they are. This recipe is inspired by one eaten thousands of years ago (carrots and cinnamon weren't Greek). Serve it with barley bread (recipe on opposite page), whole wheat, or pita bread.

Makes 4 Servings

8 ounces (236 g) green lentils

3 cups (705 ml) low-sodium chicken broth

2 small leeks, white parts only, chopped, or 4 scallions

2 carrots, peeled and chopped

1/2 teaspoon (1.5 g) turmeric

1/2 teaspoon (1.1 g) cinnamon

2 tablespoons (30 ml) apple cider vinegar

1 tablespoon (15 ml) honey

Salt and pepper

1 tablespoon (15 ml) olive oil

1 Place the lentils in a bowl and cover with cold water; soak overnight. The next day, rinse and place in a large saucepan. Cover with cold water, an inch above the lentils. Ask an adult to turn the heat on to medium; cook, simmering gently, for 20 minutes.

2 Add in all the remaining ingredients except the olive oil and cook for 10 minutes more or until the carrots and lentils are tender. Drizzle with the olive oil before serving. Then start your warm-up exercises for the Olympics!

> " Lentils make any meal tasty and healthy. "
> Mena, 12

HIPPOCRATES' FAVORITE BARLEY BREAD

Barley, believed by the Greeks to be a gift from the goddess Demeter, was a staple. This version, loosely adapted from the beloved *The Tassajara Bread Book* by Edward Espe Brown, will have a very tough crust with a dense but tender crumb. While sunflower seeds are a New World ingredient, they give the bread a nutty flavor.

Makes 4 Servings

5 teaspoons (70 ml) toasted sesame oil

2 cups (296 g) barley flour

4 cups (452 g) whole wheat flour

3/4 cups (105 g) roasted sunflower seeds, preferably unsalted

1-1/2 teaspoons (8 g) salt

2 tablespoons (30 ml) sunflower oil, plus a little to grease loaf pan

3-1/2 cups (830 ml) water

1 Ask an adult to heat the sesame oil in a medium skillet over medium-high heat. Add the barley flour and cook until darkened, about 2 minutes. (Reduce heat if it starts to burn.)

2 In a large bowl, combine the whole wheat flour, sunflower seeds, and salt, and then add the barley flour and mix well with a large spoon.

3 Add the sunflower oil to the flour mixture and mix until it's fully incorporated and the flour becomes oily.

4 Ask an adult to help you boil 3-1/2 cups water, and then pour the boiling water into the bowl, 1 cup at a time, while you gently mix with a large spoon to form a wet, sticky dough.

5 On a lightly floured surface, knead the dough by hand, pushing and pulling the dough, until smooth, approximately 10 minutes. (Your hands will be so strong by the end of this!)

6 Grease a bread pan with some oil. Shape the dough into a loaf and place it in the bread pan. Make a deep cut lengthwise down the loaf. Place in a warm spot and let rest for 8 hours or overnight.

7 Ask an adult to preheat the oven to 450°F/230°C and bake for 25 minutes. Then reduce heat to 400°F/200°C and bake for an additional 30 minutes or more, until the crust is nice and dark.

" It's like a softer, more flavorful cracker. "
Cameron, 15

POPCORNY quiz

1

What was a favorite snack in Greece?

A. Popcorn
B. Lungs of a blue-footed booby
C. Pasta with tomato sauce
D. Honey and nuts
E. Chicken nostrils

2

Around what age were kids in ancient Greece considered adults?

A. 7
B. 3
C. 45
D. 13
E. 29

3

Which food did the Greeks rarely eat?

A. Snails
B. Raisins
C. Pork
D. Lamb
E. Eel

4

What material didn't they use to keep their ovens going?

A. Olive wood
B. Oak wood
C. Sheep poop
D. Cow poop
E. Beech wood

5

Which of these things was always present at mealtime?

A. Water
B. Forks
C. Plates
D. Tablecloths
E. Bread

6

What wasn't used as a napkin?

A. A napkin
B. The diner's tunic
C. Bread
D. A tablecloth
E. The diner's hand

Those Greeks sure knew how to have an eel-y good time!

7

Who ran the first marathon?

A. Pheidippides
B. Seidippides
C. Teidippides
D. Leidippides
E. Meidippides

A six-by-four-foot (1.8-by-1.2-m) clay tablet inscribed with **25 meat** and **vegetable recipes** from **1750** B.C. was found by scientists. A cookbook in clay form!

Rome:
Chariots, Circuses, and Roast Cranes

A BITE-SIZE history

W hile the Greeks were busy dreaming up math, philosophy, and medicine, across the Adriatic Sea, another world empire was emerging.

Rome is a *bellissimo* (beautiful) city located on seven hills in central Italy, and it sure wasn't built in a day, as the saying goes. But 2,000 years ago, Rome wasn't just a city—it was the center of the Roman Republic and then the Roman Empire. Beginning officially in 509 B.C. and lasting until A.D. 1453, this empire ruled more than 60 million people, or 20 percent of the world's population, at the height of its power. It stretched from Asia Minor (what is now Turkey) and northern Africa all the way across most of Europe to Britain. Guess what language they spoke? Nope, not Italian! They actually spoke Latin and some Greek.

According to myth, twin brothers Romulus and Remus, sons of the god Mars, founded a settlement in 735 B.C. Romulus then killed his brother and became king of a place named after him: Rome. Other kings followed until King Lucius Tarquinius Superbus (we didn't make that name up) was run out of Rome by his nephew, Lucius Junius Brutus, in 509 B.C. At that point, the citizens declared Rome a republic, in which citizens were in charge and represented by their elected officials.

Its government was ruled by two consuls elected each year by a senate of wealthy citizens; Brutus was elected one of the first two consuls. The consuls ran the army as well as the government. Eventually common people (called plebeians) complained long enough that they got their own officials elected to a tribune of the plebs, which balanced the power of the senate. (The United States' system of government is partly based on Rome's model, with three divisions of power, including a senate.)

ROME'S COLOSSEUM

Present-day boundaries are shown.

ITALY

Rome

Adriatic Sea

One key ingredient for building a powerful government? Establishing cities. Romans were expert architects and engineers, and they used concrete to build magnificent cities, especially their capital, Rome. One of their biggest efforts was the enormous Roman Forum, a public plaza with temples and government buildings surrounding it. The Romans also built the Circus Maximus, an enormous stadium that could hold more than 150,000 people, and the Colosseum, which held 50,000 (the ruins of all three remain major tourist attractions today).

Hungry for power and riches, Roman Republic leaders conquered huge swaths of land in Europe and beyond. To connect the republic's newly conquered peoples, Roman soldiers, with help from enslaved subjects, constructed 50,000 miles (80,467 km) of highways and bridges, as well as other important public works like aqueducts to deliver water, spas to bathe in, and sewer systems.

Leaders of the Roman Republic also tried to create a common culture. The republic had the first newspaper, known as *Acta Diurna*, which was carved in stone or metal. A common currency with rulers' profiles stamped on coins was used. They developed a postal system and a set of laws, many of which are the basis for laws used in the United States today, including the concept that people are

A ROMAN BATTLE

innocent until proven guilty and should receive equal treatment under the law.

But the republic faced many challenges, including a famous one in 218 B.C. when Hannibal and his Carthaginian army (who lived in what is now Tunisia) crossed the Alps with a massive army, including 38 war elephants, to attack the Roman Republic. Hannibal had initially tried to take over Spain, which was allied with Rome, but he was eventually beaten back by the Roman Army.

Battles within the republic's territories were nearly constant because it was just so huge and rich. Probably the most famous Roman leader was Julius Caesar, an ambitious military leader who conquered parts of Britain in 54 B.C. and, as we already know, Egypt in 47 B.C.

But absolute power can corrupt absolutely, and Caesar began to act like a dictator. He held epic gladiator contests with horse-drawn chariots. He forced a battle between 2,000 prisoners, 200 horses, and 20 elephants. He flooded land in Rome to stage pretend naval battles with dozens of ships. He was declared dictator for life. But on March 15, 44 B.C., he was stabbed to death by 60 senators.

> " You should pray for a **healthy mind** in a healthy body. "
>
> Roman poet Juvenal

Caesar's nephew took over next, and the Roman Republic became the Roman Empire, ending its citizen-elected government. Then, in A.D. 275, the Roman Empire split into two separate governments. The Western Roman Empire governed what is now France, Spain, Belgium, Britain, Italy, and other parts of Europe; it lasted until 410, when the city of Rome was taken over by the northern Visigoth tribe, which weakened the Western empire, and led to its official end in 476. The Byzantine, or Eastern Roman Empire, included, at times, what is now Turkey, Greece, Egypt, North Africa, and other areas, and lasted until 1453.

The Roman Empire turned out to be one of the most powerful and high-achieving empires in history. Maybe its great food had something to do with all those accomplishments?

A ROMAN KITCHEN SERVANT

A DAY in the Life: Rome, 30 B.C.

"*Bonum mane.*" Good morning. Whether in a six-story wood-and-mud-brick apartment building or a simple three-room mud-brick home, people rose with the sun. Children might have left their small wooden beds; slipped on their *togas* (one long piece of draped linen), their *soccus* (socks) when it was cold, and necklaces with a *bulla* or *lunula* (protective charms); and sat down to breakfast, either in the kitchen, the courtyard, or the dining room.

Mater (Latin for "mom") usually cooked every meal, except in wealthy homes where slaves cooked everything. Poorer families had gruel for breakfast—wheat flour mixed with water, and sometimes salt and olive oil. Wealthier families had big healthy breakfasts of dried fruit, bread, cooked eggs, cheese, and sheep or goat's milk.

Then it was time for kids to study, work, or play. Only well-to-do boys over seven went to school. Everyone else learned Latin at home, as well as basic reading, writing, and math. Kids also helped with whatever jobs their parents had and gathered food from the garden, fields, streams, or market. One typical chore was taking grain to the local baker to have him bake the bread—only rich families baked their own at home.

Prandium, also known as lunch, was a quick meal, such as cooked and cooled veggies drizzled in olive oil, salad greens, bread, and grapes—kind of similar to what students may bring to school for lunch nowadays.

After finishing the day's chores—which included sewing, weaving, cooking, and cleaning for girls; going to the market for boys—it was playtime, which might include piggyback, tag, juggling, and playing basketball with pig bladders. Then it was time for *cena*, or dinner. Stew or pottage was a common dish, with roots like turnips and onions, as well as cabbage, lentils, chickpeas, favas, and anything else that could be thrown into the pot. The stew was served with bread. Because the poor received a grain allotment from the government, many people ate a lot of bread.

Luckier families with enough money could buy spices to use in their dinner; some spices, like cinnamon and pepper, came all the way from India. After dinner, it was back to bed to dream of chariot races, the NASCAR of its day, and far-flung Roman outposts to visit, only to repeat that same basic schedule the next day.

Spicing Things Up!

The Romans believed that you are what you eat, so one of the world's greatest empires was built on veggies. Many homes had their own walled gardens, and fresh produce was part of every meal. Romans preserved food at the end of the growing season by pickling, drying, curing, and smoking it, or storing it in honey—meat preserved with honey can last up to four years. Preserving was another job children helped with.

Fresh fish was as close as the nearby stream, river, or sea and very popular. The Romans loved fish so much they perfected aquaculture, which China had invented to raise farms of oysters, snails, mussels, and freshwater fish.

City dwellers got much of their food at the macellum, or market, either weekly or daily. One of the largest markets in Rome was the two-story Trajan's Market, one of the world's first malls. It had 150 shops and offices in an enormous complex, and its ruins still stand today.

Food was prepared in either indoor kitchens —which featured hooks for hanging tools and cupboards that held plates, cups, glasses, and mortars and pestles—or courtyards.

Richer homes had a *furnus*—a brick, stone, or clay oven that burned twigs or charcoal (some even had two ovens!). But most people got by with covered charcoal braziers to grill, boil, or sauté their food.

A FIRST-CENTURY BAKERY IN POMPEII

Table matters!

Pater (Latin for "father"), or the eldest male, sat at the head of the table and received the best food and service. Tables were usually wooden; some had adjustable legs to make them shorter or taller. Most people sat on stools, benches, or mats, but some wealthy people ate lying down on couches grouped around a table with heaps of glorious food.

At these wealthy, formal dinners, adults removed their sandals, washed their hands and feet, and then lay on a couch to begin the gluttony. Hopefully they remembered to bring spoons, which weren't provided, and their napkins, which were also used to bring home leftovers. No plastic containers or baggies then!

When a guest asked for **his sandals** after dinner, that was the cue that **he was ready to leave.**

Common foods eaten in Rome at the time:

- Salted fish
- Geese
- Cranes
- Pork
- Snails
- Oysters
- Figs
- Grapes
- Honey
- Leeks
- Pine nuts
- Chestnuts
- Peaches
- Hard cheeses
- Lentils
- Broad beans
- Barley

Servants prepare a Roman feast in this second-century A.D. mosaic.

ROMAN
Kitchen Tools

AS THE ROMANS WERE ONE OF THE MOST ADVANCED SOCIETIES IN EUROPEAN HISTORY, IT'S NO SURPRISE THEY USED RESOURCEFUL TOOLS:

Tongs

These claspers were used to pull food items out of boiling water or fire.

Knives

No more ripping apart food with hands at the dinner table! Diners were expected to use knives for serving and cutting meat.

Caccabus Braziers

An ingenious mini grill that had movable rods, it could grill everything from tiny snails to big pork chops.

Pasta Machines

Pasta-making devices were used to create thin, wide, flat pasta strips like the ones that went into Roman politician Consul Cicero's favorite dish: *laganum*. This is called lasagna today!

The senator and historian Cato recommended that sick people eat lots of cabbage and then bathe in their own urine to get better.

Romans mixed days-old human urine with water to wash their togas; some cloth manufacturers set up urinals to get more "cleanser" for their work.

Some rich nobles displayed their wealth by throwing away entire slabs of beef—a luxury food—into the Tiber River during banquets.

MENUS OF THE
Rich & Famished

At parties, many dishes were served, from cheeses and olives to lamb, shrimp, and peaches. Rich hosts who really wanted to impress their guests served the biggest, fattest dormice they could get their hands on. Nothing like a roasted rodent to get the party started! Pork bones, oyster shells, shrimp tails, and anything else the guests couldn't eat were thrown on the floor. Slaves provided the entertainment, which was usually singing, dancing, or acrobatics.

At one party, Emperor Vitellius served a huge silver dish with the empire's most exotic foods—char livers, pheasant and peacock brains, flamingo tongues, and the entrails of lampreys.

One Roman general, Lucullus, dined extravagantly each day, whether alone or with guests. He once spent the equivalent of several million dollars on one dinner with two politicians.

Julius Caesar celebrated one of his military victories by serving 2,000 moray eels.

WHAT DID FOOD COST IN 301 B.C.?
This is what an aristocrat might spend on a feast. (All prices are in the currency *denarius communis*, and 1 D.C. was about equal to one day's pay for a farmer or laborer.)

cabbage, 1 D.C.	olive oil, 40 D.C.
peaches, 1 D.C.	chicken, 60 D.C.
freshwater fish, 12 D.C.	salt, 100 D.C.
pork, 12 D.C.	lentils, 100 D.C.
goat, 12 D.C.	rice, 200 D.C.
saltwater fish, 25 D.C.	goose, fattened 200 D.C.

A ROMAN EMPIRE SOLDIER'S DAILY PORTION OF FOOD:
2 pounds (0.9 kg) of wheat, 6 ounces (170 g) of meat, 1-1/2 ounces (42.5 g) of lentils, 1 ounce (28 g) of cheese, 1-1/2 ounces (44 ml) of olive oil , 6 ounces (177 ml) of vinegar, 1-1/2 ounces (42.5 g) of salt, 1/2 gallon (2 L) of water

3,000 POUNDS OF PEPPER:
One of the gifts the Visigoths demanded when they conquered the Western Roman Empire in the fifth century A.D.

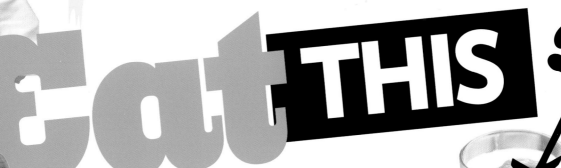

Eat THIS

APICIUS' APRICOT DELIGHT

This is adapted from a 1,600-year-old recipe found in the fourth-century *Cooking and Dining in Imperial Rome,* written by one of the world's first cookbook authors, Apicius. Any stone fruit, like plums, nectarines, or peaches, can be used in place of apricots. One recipe tester recommends adding a pinch of nutmeg and cinnamon.

Makes 2 Servings

4 fresh apricots—peeled, pitted, and quartered

1 cup (237 ml) milk

2 tablespoons (30 ml) honey

Freshly ground pepper

1 cup (244 g) vanilla Greek yogurt

Butter, for greasing pan

1 In a large bowl, combine the apricots, milk, honey, and pepper (yes, we said pepper). Stir and let sit for half an hour.

2 Ask an adult to preheat the oven to 350°F/177°C. Grease a nonstick baking pan with sides, such as a 13 x 9 inch (33 x 23 cm) pan, or a nonstick loaf pan. Drain the apricots and transfer to the pan. Ask an adult to put the pan in the oven. Bake for 40 minutes or until the apricots are mushy and soft. Ask an adult to remove the pan from the oven. Stir, divide among 2 bowls, and top each with 1/2 cup of yogurt.

❝ I know it seems like letting the ingredients sit for half an hour is going to take forever, but it is worth the wait. ❞
Aliana, 13

HAIL CAESAR CHICKEN SALAD

While Caesar salad wasn't invented by the Romans (it was actually invented in Mexico in 1924 by Caesar Cardini, an Italian who lived in the United States and Mexico), salad greens, cheese, and bread were three indispensable Roman ingredients. So even if they didn't invent Ceasar salad, we are sure they would have loved it! We're adding chicken for extra protein and spinach for bonus nutrients, but you can substitute shrimp for the chicken or skip it altogether.

1 Ask an adult to warm 1 tablespoon olive oil in a large sauté pan over medium heat. Add the chicken and cook for 5 minutes on each side, or until cooked. Let cool, then chop into bite-size pieces.

2 Rub the inside of a large salad bowl with the peeled garlic (use a wooden salad bowl if you can, as that will absorb the flavor of the garlic the most). Discard the garlic. Into the bowl, add the lemon juice, vinegar, anchovy paste if you are using it, mustard, and the remaining 1/4 cup olive oil; whisk until blended.

3 Slice the romaine lengthwise (stopping at the stem) and then crosswise into half-inch-wide strips. Add the lettuce and spinach to the salad bowl and toss.

4 Add the chicken, sprinkle with the cheese, and season with salt and pepper to taste.

Makes 4 Servings

1/4 cup plus 1 tablespoon (70 ml) olive oil

1 medium boneless skinless chicken breast

1 large garlic clove, peeled and halved

Juice of 1/4 fresh lemon

1-1/2 tablespoons (30 ml) red wine or apple cider vinegar

1/2 teaspoon (5 g) anchovy paste (optional)

1/2 teaspoon (2.5 g) Dijon mustard

1 small head romaine lettuce

1 cup (30 g) spinach

2 tablespoons (10 g) grated Parmigiano-Reggiano cheese

Salt and pepper

" I think this would be a great salad to take on a picnic. "
Sydney, 16

POP CORNY
quiz

1

Before bathing in his own urine to cure sickness, a Roman would eat lots of:

A. Chicken beaks
B. Snails
C. Cabbage
D. Lampreys
E. Pig trotters

2

What did it mean if a dinner guest asked for his or her sandals?

A. They wanted to have them cleaned.
B. They were going to use them to catch a fish.
C. They wanted a piggyback.
D. They were ready to leave the party.
E. It was code for grant me a wish.

3

When Romans went to a dinner party, they brought their:

A. Napkins
B. Pet eel
C. Mobile phone
D. Credit cards
E. Spaghetti

4

What ingredient was rare and mostly consumed by the rich?

A. Olives
B. Geese
C. Apricots
D. Cranes
E. Beef

5

What too was found in almost every Roman kitchen?

A. Tongs
B. Mortar and pestle
C. Knife
D. Brazier
E. All of the above

6

How many shops and offices did Trajan's Market have?

A. 2
B. 17
C. 37.5
D. 99
E. 150

Did somebody say "ruff"?

7

What did Romans do to display their wealth?

A. Threw a Fourth of July fireworks show
B. Threw sides of beef into a river
C. Dressed up in chicken suits
D. Dipped themselves in gold leaf
E. Refused to speak to anyone but their dog

Medieval
Times:
Barbarians, Braised Peacock, and
Damsels Sometimes in Distress

A BITE-SIZE history

Medieval times in Europe, also called the Middle Ages, lasted from the fifth to 14th century. It was an era of crusaders, peasants, knights, castles, cathedrals, and a mysterious disease that killed more than half of Europe's population.

In the fifth century, the Western Roman Empire had disintegrated into smaller states ruled by numerous tribes that the Romans referred to as "barbarians" because they didn't speak Greek or Latin. The nomadic Hun tribe took over what is now Germany, Hungary, and parts of Russia; the Persian Empire ruled what's now the Middle East and Central Asia.

The empire wouldn't be united again until a new conqueror took charge in the 790s. His name was Charlemagne, and his rise marked the reunification of much of the Western Roman Empire. Charlemagne forcibly spread Christianity by executing thousands who refused to convert. In gratitude, Pope Leo III, the head of the Catholic Church, declared Charlemagne the "Holy Roman Emperor" on Christmas Day in 800. Charlemagne and his heirs ruled an enormous Christian empire into the 900s. Part of their army included armored soldiers called knights. In return for their service in battle, these brave, rich aristocrats were rewarded with land, castles, palaces, and titles. Knights often became famous and beloved.

Around the same time Charlemagne established his empire, Vikings in Norway, Denmark, and Sweden were exploring the world in their long ships. From the ninth to the 12th century, they pillaged, conquered, raided, and traded all over parts of Europe, Russia, and the Middle East. One notorious Viking was Erik the Red, who lived in Iceland until he was banished for murder. In 982, he fled to the land next door, which he called Greenland despite the fact it was all ice. (He hoped

EMPEROR CHARLEMAGNE

to entice others to join him—talk about false advertising!) Erik's son, Leif Eriksson, known as Leif the Lucky, sailed from Greenland to North America around 1000, and explored what is now Newfoundland in Canada, making him the first known European explorer to visit North America. Meanwhile, Charlemagne's empire steadily collapsed throughout the 900s, and kings and queens began to reign over France, Spain, and England. Europe's countries, borders, and capitals started to resemble the Europe we know today. During this feudal society, as it's now known, between the ninth and 15th centuries, there was very little movement in social classes: Someone born a peasant likely stayed a peasant. Kings and queens were at the tip-top, followed by nobles such as lords and ladies, then knights, then the clergy, then tradespeople, and finally peasants.

Peasants made up 90 percent of the population and had to take an oath of obedience and loyalty to their lords. They could not leave their village or even marry without their lord's permission. Peasants had to pay to use their lord's mill to grind flour or his oven to bake bread; they worked his lands or in his household at least three days each week. Life for peasants was very hard and few lived past the age of 35.

Beginning in 1088, Pope Urban II asked for volunteers all over Europe to help remove the Muslim military forces that had occupied Jerusalem since 637. Thousands of Christians, some of them knights and some peasants, joined a series of

GREENLAND

ICELAND

NORWAY

UNITED KINGDOM

SWEDEN

IRELAND Dublin

London

DENMARK

RUSSIA

GERMANY

Paris

FRANCE

HUNGARY

SPAIN

Present-day boundaries are shown.

DOES LEIF ERIKSSON LOOK LUCKY?

bloody Crusades that continued for the next 200 years. One famous crusader, Richard the Lionheart, was King of England for 10 years (1189–1199), yet only spent a total of six months in his country. He complained it was cold and always raining.

In 1215, King John of England created the Magna Carta. It was the world's first constitution and went on to inspire many government documents, including America's Bill of Rights. The Magna Carta established that no one, from king on down, was above the law.

In the 1300s, Europe experienced two terrible disasters: the Great Famine, which began in 1315 and led to the starvation of at least 10 percent of Europe's population, and the Black Death, which began in 1347 and was a plague carried by fleas and rodents that killed upward of 200 million people.

> "Whoso will keep **continual health**, keep his stomach so that he **put not too much therein when he hath appetite**, nor take anything into it when he **hath no need**. And then **continual health will ensue.**"
>
> *Bald's Leechbook*, A.D. 950s

And yet, it wasn't all doom and gloom. So many items we use today—eyeglasses, mechanical clocks, windmills, gunpowder and handheld guns, and even buttons—were invented during the second half of the Middle Ages. Books like Chaucer's *Canterbury Tales* and the spectacularly illustrated *Book of Kells*, which is still on display in Dublin, Ireland, were written. Then there were the entrancing tales of knights, such as King Arthur and the Knights of the Round Table. These armored soldiers were depicted not just in battle but at court demonstrating their dedication to the Code of Chivalry, which promoted bravery, honor, dignity, and protection of women. One of the greatest achievements of the second half of the Middle Ages was the construction of spectacular stone castles and cathedrals. Many, such as the Tower of London and Paris's Notre Dame, can be visited today.

So what did people eat during the Middle Ages?

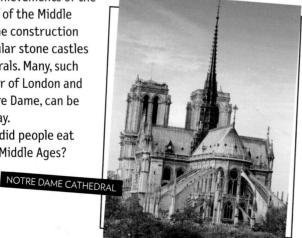

NOTRE DAME CATHEDRAL

A DAY in the Life: England, 1450

Cold—so very cold. That's how it might have felt waking up in England on a straw mattress covered with a woolen blanket in a two-room cottage situated on a lord's land.

After getting up, kids might let the animals outside; these weren't pets but farm animals that provided the family's clothing, food, and plowing needs. During the winter, sheep, chickens, goats, and other animals often slept inside cottages for warmth. Imagine the smell and noise when everyone was trying to sleep! *Baaaaaa!* Luckily, many households threw straw, herbs, and flowers on the floor to help with the stench and absorb some of the mess.

Children wore rough woolen clothes even in summer (unless they were wealthy, in which case they put on linen, silk, or velvet). Clothing was generally really dirty as it was washed only once each spring. Older boys wore long socks, short pants, and a shirt; if they were younger than 10, they wore a long dress of sorts. Girls wore plain long-sleeved dresses. Breakfast, usually prepared by mom, was either barley porridge or barley pancakes.

There were few schools, so most kids did not know how to read or write. Noble boys seven and older might train to become a knight, practicing how to put on heavy armor and to joust atop a horse. Other boys apprenticed with their fathers or worked on their lord's manor. Or they helped at the stables, working with newly invented horseshoes, stirrups, and bridles, as well as knights' armor. Girls learned to cook, clean, garden, and take care of the animals. They also spun wool into yarn for clothing. The family would stop around midday to eat what they called dinner, the largest meal of the day.

After dinner and chores, kids played games like knucklebones, a primitive version of jacks, and ran around. Snacks consisted of fruit or old, crusty bread. Supper, usually eaten at dusk, was leftovers from dinner. There was no bath time—most people bathed only a few times a year, probably around Easter, June, September, and Christmas.

Kids would bring in the animals and hit the hay, literally, at 7 or 8 p.m., as they'd be getting up early to do all their chores again tomorrow. Time to blow out the candles, knights and damsels.

Spicing Things Up!

What people ate depended entirely on how much money or land they had. There was little trading, and poorly maintained roads made it difficult to reach the few markets that operated. Those that did exist were in bigger cities, and they had fishmongers, bakers, butchers, and grain merchants. Wild animals ran freely through city streets, so sometimes it was hard to get to the market because a cow was in the way!

Most people ate whatever grew, ran, flew, or swam near them. But bad harvests, plagues, and floods made it hard to grow or raise a lot of foods. Barley was one exception, as it grows easily in many different soils and weather.

Because nobles didn't do any heavy labor, and thus didn't need that much strength, doctors believed they should eat lighter foods such as fish and chicken; peasants were told to eat harder-to-digest meats like boar and goat to give them energy and strength.

In peasant homes, the kitchen was simply some pots over the fireplace. A lord and lady's manor house, which also served as the administrative center for the village, had a separate kitchen with a large hearth to cook over and several rooms for aging meats and cheeses and drying spices and herbs. Castles and monasteries had the most impressive kitchens, with large staffs tending fires, milling flour, baking loaves of bread in multiple ovens, and butchering meat.

Table matters!

Royals and nobles in late medieval times ate multiple dishes at dinner while everyone else had one, most likely a stew served in a trencher —a hollowed-out piece of bread that doubled as a bowl. Everyone ate together, but in big manors or castles seating was dictated by a person's station in society. The fanciest folks sat higher at a raised table or stage, which put them within reach of the salt, a condiment that was rare and expensive. No one began eating until everyone was served, and the lord always took the first bite. And sometimes, people came just to watch the royals eat.

Guests either brought wooden spoons and steel knives with them (tucked into boots if they were men) or just used their left hands to eat. Those who could afford them had earthenware dishes, and everyone shared goblets.

In most homes tables were moved to the side when supper was done, as there wasn't enough space for them to stay in the middle of the room. Those who didn't have a table sat around the hearth.

Common foods eaten during medieval times:

- Cabbage
- Mushrooms
- Cauliflower
- Apples
- Chickpeas
- Lentils
- Oats
- Rye
- Barley
- Venison
- Lamb
- Boar
- Pork
- Honey
- Goat cheese
- Almond milk
- Fish

In King Edward IV's court in England, one **person's full-time job** was to **make the king waffles.**

A knight's armor was made just for him—and his beloved horse.

MEDIEVAL
Kitchen Tools

THE MIDDLE AGES WERE NOT A TIME FOR SNAZZY INVENTIONS. SOME NEW TOOLS INCLUDED:

LE VIANDIER COOKBOOK

Water Mills

According to the *Domesday Book*, which had a record of all of England's households in 1086, there was one water mill for every 50 families. Powered by a waterwheel, the mill ground flour in minutes instead of an hour.

Cookbooks

Le Viandier was written around 1300 by Taillevent, who was the master cook for Charles V, king of France. It became a favorite of master chefs across Europe, and it was so popular that 24 editions had been published by 1615.

To keep butter from going bad, cooks in wealthy northern European homes salted it so heavily that it had to be rinsed before being used.

Some bakers whitened their flour with ground bones or chalk; any baker caught doing so in England or France was punished by being locked in a pillory (a wooden framework with holes for the head and hands) with a loaf of bread hanging from his neck.

THE PILLORY WAS A PUNISHMENT DEVICE.

MENUS OF THE
Rich & Famished

During the 14th and 15th centuries, the rich and royal had ice brought down from mountaintops and stored in the basements of their cold, damp castles to be shaved and served with honey to impress their guests. Another "wow" item was braised peacock, served standing up, breathing fire out of its mouth (fabric was stuffed in its mouth and ignited).

Hosts sat either at a separate table on a stage above the crowd or in the middle of a U-shaped tablecloth-covered table. Waiters loudly announced each dish as it was presented because there were no printed menus. (Imagine mom coming in and yelling "Spinach pie!" at the dinner table tonight.) Fruit was served first, followed by pottages (stews), roasts, tarts, pastries and pies, and finally wafers, cheese, and candied fruits.

After a feast given by the Count of Anjou, son of King Louis II of Sicily, in 1455, you'd think few animals were left to be eaten! The first course consisted of hare, a quarter of a stag, a stuffed chicken, and veal. The next course featured 2 pies made with 1 deer, 1 gosling, 3 roosters, 6 chickens, 10 pigeons, and 1 rabbit. The next courses consisted of roast deer, pig, sturgeon, goat, 2 goslings, 12 chickens, 12 pigeons, 6 rabbits, 2 herons, 1 fat rooster, 4 chickens covered with egg yolks and sprinkled with spice, and a wild boar. Room for dessert? There were wafers, cream, cheese, strawberries, plums stewed in rosewater, fruit preserves, and sweet pastries, some of which included the expensive ingredient sugar.

By the Numbers

164,000: Eels fished out of the Count of Flanders's pond in 1187, near what is the Netherlands today.

17: Courses at the wedding of Duke Lionel of Clarence in 1368—16 of which were meat. The first course was "gilded, fire-eating pork, and gilded sea snail."

74: Varieties of veggies, herbs, and fruits Emperor Charlemagne cultivated in his gardens in Aachen (now Germany).

17: Number of grams of the rare and precious spice saffron that could buy an entire horse.

172: Cooks and other staff needed to create the feast for George Neville upon his becoming Archbishop of York in 1466.

Cheese was so valued in Germany that it could be used to pay rent.

Eat THIS

ALMOND MILK
FOR LORDS AND LADIES

This recipe is inspired by one from the fascinating *The Medieval Kitchen,* in which author Hannele Klemettilä features an almond milk recipe from the 14th-century cookbook *Le Viandier.* Almond milk was popular because it didn't require refrigeration, unlike cow's milk.

Makes 4 Servings

1 cup (140 g) almonds

3 cups (711 ml) water, plus extra for step 1

2 teaspoons (10 ml) maple syrup or honey

1 teaspoon (5 ml) vanilla extract

1/2 teaspoon (2.5 g) salt

1 Finely grind the almonds in a food processor or high-speed blender. Transfer to a large bowl and add enough water to cover the almonds.

2 Add another 3 cups of water, maple syrup, vanilla, and salt and blend about 2 minutes, or until thoroughly blended.

3 Over a large measuring cup, place a sieve lined with a fine cheesecloth, thin dish towel, or nut milk bag. Pour the blended mixture through the cheesecloth into the cup. Gather up the cheesecloth, and squeeze tightly, extracting as much milk from the bag as possible. Drink up! Cover and refrigerate any milk you don't drink right away. Discard the nut pulp in the bag.

" This would be good in smoothies. "
Jacob, 14

KING ARTHUR'S PUMPES IN A TRENCHER

Pork meatballs *(pumpes)* in almond milk was a popular dish in the Middle Ages. This recipe is adapted from a book published around 1450 called *Two Fifteenth-Century Cookery-Books*. Serve it on a trencher—a hollowed-out crusty piece of bread that doubles as a bowl. You could use ground turkey or chicken in place of the pork; the recipe's original author said that you can use veal or beef but that he thinks pork is best.

1 Ask an adult to preheat the oven to 375°F/190°C. In a large bowl, thoroughly mix the pork with the eggs, bread crumbs, raisins, 1/2 teaspoon salt, and cinnamon. Roll into small 2-inch meatballs and place on a large baking pan or sheet lined with aluminum foil. Ask an adult to transfer to the oven and cook for 30 minutes or until golden brown.

2 In the last 5 minutes of cooking, add the trenchers (recipe at right) to the oven to warm them. Ask an adult to remove the meatball pumpes from the oven.

3 Ask an adult to warm the almond milk in a large stockpot over medium heat. Gently stir in the flour and a pinch of salt and stir. Add the meatball pumpes and let cook for 2 minutes.

4 Ask an adult to remove the trenchers from the oven. Spoon the meatball pumpes with the milk into each trencher and serve.

Makes 4 Servings

1-1/2 pounds (675 g) ground pork

2 eggs

2/3 cup (60 g) plain, dried unseasoned bread crumbs

1/2 cup (75 g) raisins

1/2 teaspoon (2.5 g) salt, plus a pinch

1 teaspoon (2.3 g) ground cinnamon

6 trenchers (see instructions below)

1 cup (237 ml) Almond Milk for Lords and Ladies or unsweetened store-bought almond milk

1/4 cup (31 g) all-purpose flour

How to Make a Trencher

Take a loaf of French bread (called a baguette) or an Italian loaf and cut it into 4 equal quarters. Cut each quarter in half lengthwise (you should have 8 pieces). Scoop out much of the bread inside, hollowing it so there is still about a half-inch-thick crust left all the way around. Toast, bake, broil, or grill (with a drizzle of olive oil or a bit of butter if you'd like), or use as is.

> " Wow. How cool. This recipe was invented 42 years before Columbus sailed the ocean blue! "
> Tim, 11

POP CORNY quiz

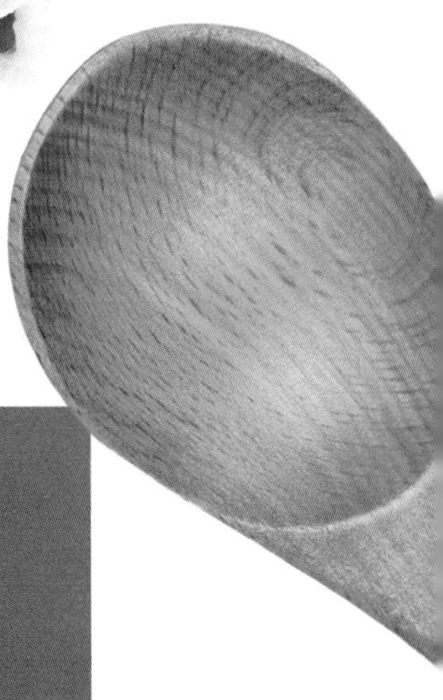

Why did people usually eat only what they caught or grew?

A. The government didn't give any money to the poor.
B. There was little trading.
C. The roads were poorly maintained.
D. There were few markets.
E. All of the above.

1

Who was the first European explorer known to reach North America?

A. Leif the Leprechaun
B. Leaf the Leaf
C. Leif the Lucky
D. Leify McLeify
E. Luff Luff

2

How many times would clothes get washed each year?

A. 1
B. 12
C. 24
D. 48
E. 365

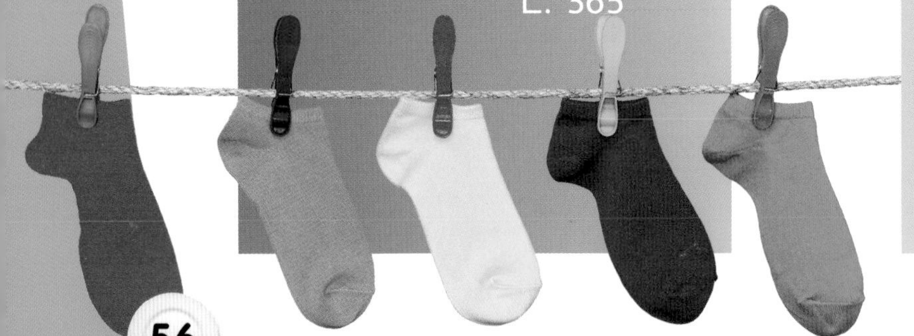

4

How did some peasants pay their rent?

A. With cheese
B. With snails
C. With shells
D. With rocks
E. With knitting

5

Anyone invited to a friend's home for supper brought:

A. Their pet goldfish
B. Their computer
C. Their long board
D. Their imaginary best friend
E. Their wooden spoon and a steel knife

At least **70 barrels of anchovies** destined for Pope Eugene IV were stolen off a ship in 1383.

In 1378, a law was passed that **no meat could be sold** in London after night fell.

In the Middle Ages, **pigs were half the size** they are today. (We bred them to be bigger in later years.)

6

To keep butter from going bad, cooks did what?

A. Put a lot of salt in it
B. Put it in the refrigerator
C. Put it in the freezer
D. Ate it as soon as they made it
E. Gave it to their dogs

Wait just a minute ...

7

What was a typical dish served at royal banquets?

A. Roast unicorn
B. Braised bear
C. Grilled bees
D. Sautéed tongue of boar
E. Cooked peacock

Mongols & the Silk Road:
Genghis, Gers, and Yogurt

A BITE-SIZE history

Imagine walking on a road made of silk. Dreamy, right? And yet the Silk Road, a 4,000-mile (6,437-km) group of trade routes connecting Europe, China, the Middle East, and North Africa, was the opposite of silky smooth. Long before the days of overnight international shipping, the muddy, bumpy Silk Road enabled the sharing of information and goods across much of the world.

EUROPE

ASIA

AFRICA

Silk Road

Present-day boundaries are shown.

The Silk Road's first trade route started thousands of years ago; we know this because some Egyptian mummies were buried with Chinese silk. The routes grew in length and number over time. By the first century B.C., China had trade routes to India and Rome; by the eighth century A.D., the network had united much of Europe and Asia, going from what's now Korea to Italy.

Traveling the Silk Road meant crossing forests, deserts, and mountaintops, and it was often very dangerous. People could be robbed or worse as they walked or rode horses or camels on the paths. But the rewards outweighed the risks because this network of economic and cultural highways spread income, customs, knowledge, and even religion—including Buddhism and Islam—to much of the world.

There was no single ruler over the Silk Road for hundreds of years. Rather, different groups from different regions presided over various parts of it, from China's Hans to the Scythians and Sogdians of Iran. As the years went by and trade increased, the routes got busier and its outposts larger. Then in the 13th century, a new group began to control all of the outposts. Meet the Mongols.

The Mongols were horseback-riding nomads who eventually controlled Central Asia, including much of China, Russia, and Persia. In fact, during their heyday, from the 13th to the 15th century, they would rule a vast empire equal to the size

GENGHIS KHAN

of Africa. It was the largest contiguous, or connected, land empire in history!

Genghis Khan was the Mongols' first and most fearless leader. About 1206 he united many nomadic tribes and founded the Mongol Empire. They began taking over large settlements on the Silk Road and beyond, killing and pillaging as they went. Genghis Khan was a brutal conqueror, but he did unite the Silk Road into one enormous Mongol-controlled empire. Wisely, he preached religious tolerance, a good move for someone who ruled an empire that included so many faiths.

In 1269, Italy's Marco Polo, a businessman and frequent traveler, journeyed to China and wrote a popular book about the civilizations he encountered. (In the book he mentions lasagna, but, contrary to popular belief, Marco Polo did not introduce pasta to Italy.)

The Silk Road became even busier and safer as the Mongols created a more organized system, with outposts called yams every 20 miles (32 km) and the world's first passports, which were worn around the neck and had a symbol that indicated how important (or not) the traveler was.

Decades after Genghis Khan died in 1227, his grandson Kublai Khan established a capital called Khanbaliq in what is now Beijing, China. He also eventually built a beautiful palace which inspired the famous 18th-century poet Samuel Taylor Coleridge to write: "In Xanadu did Kubla Khan a stately pleasure-dome decree ..."

The Mongols were hardy souls, but they weren't immune to the diseases that spread via the Silk Road, especially the Black Death. Scientists think the plague started in China or Central Asia in the early 1300s and traveled via infected fleas and rodents along the Silk Road. By 1347, half of all Europeans had died from the disease.

With the death of so many in the Mongol Empire, the Mongols became less of a force. The former nomads gradually settled in lands that are now Mongolia and China. The Silk Road was fading, and once Portugal's sailors developed safer and faster sea routes in the 1500s, its importance diminished even more.

But the transformation that the Silk Road made possible was permanent, especially when it came to the spreading and blending of different types of cuisine!

> " **Conquer** one with your **hands**,
> a thousand with your **head**. "
> **Mongolian proverb**

MODERN-DAY YURT

Some Mongol warriors loved their **horses** so much they were **buried** with them.

MONGOLIAN KIDS OFTEN LOOKED AFTER EACH OTHER.

A STATUE OF KUBLAI KHAN

A DAY
in the Life:
Mongolia, 1210

Young Mongols living in what is now Mongolia might have woken up in a *ger* (or yurt) on cold, high grasslands, also called steppes. These large circular felt structures looked a bit like circus tents and were held up by wooden poles. Everyone was warmed by a fire started with dried animal poop; collecting that poop might have been a kid's job after they woke up and had breakfast.

Everyone likely wore the same clothes they slept in, usually a wool caftan (or long flowing robe) and pants. No one washed themselves because Genghis Khan believed bad spirits lived in the rivers and streams, so dishes, clothes, and people couldn't be cleaned. After having tea, yogurt, and cheese for breakfast, the tribe, which might include as few as 10 and as many as hundreds of people, would pack up the ger and gear and load it all onto yaks, camels, and wagons to travel to the next spot on the Silk Road. Sometimes that was a trading post, or sometimes just a good patch of field for the animals and tribe. Mongols constantly moved to trade and sell with others and to find good grasses for their animals to graze on.

Every day was spent traveling, sometimes going as fast as eight miles an hour (13 km/h) on horseback. All boys learned to ride and herd horses from a young age so that they were skilled horsemen by the time they became soldiers at 15. When men got married, their brides' tribes gave them horses and other animals, so it was important for men to know how to take care of them. Girls helped their mothers cook; gather food; sew clothes, hats, and gers; and take care of younger children. Kids didn't learn to read or write, but they were taught the Mongols' customs and traditions.

At the end of the day, tribal leaders would locate the perfect spot to camp for the night. The ger would get set up, which sometimes took two hours, while cooking began. Dinner varied according to the season, but it often included *buuz*, or steamed meat dumplings.

It was a tiring, difficult life, but as kids went to sleep in their warm ger and smoke rose out of the hole in its roof, they might dream about the next stop on the Silk Road and what they would find there.

Spicing Things Up!

The Mongol diet was mainly a mix of Chinese and Russian cuisines and included horse meat, mutton (older lamb), dumplings, and kumiss, or mare's milk. Mongols believed in dividing their food by color. In summer and fall, they ate mostly white dairy-based foods, including yogurt, cheese, and the fermented milk called kefir, which is popular today. In winter and spring, red foods, which were mostly meats, were eaten. Grains, fruits, and veggies rarely appeared on the menu. Because they traveled nonstop, they weren't in one place long enough to plant crops. Also, vegetables were considered food for goats. Boy, did they miss out!

Mongols didn't have to trade for or buy bacon, as it, and plenty of other "meat," traveled with them. Pigs, camels, yaks, sheep, goats, game, and cattle were part of the nomadic clan. When meat was needed, an animal was slaughtered and butchered. Exotic items like spices were traded or bought along the Silk Road.

Where did they cook up the meat and dumplings? Wherever they settled for the night. They had the ultimate mobile kitchens!

Table matters!

When people went into the ger to eat—always without their swords, bows, or other weapons—they walked in and used the greeting *nohio horio*— or hold the dog—which was their version of "hello."

Family sat to the right of the stove and guests to the left. People were served according to their rank, so kids got the last and coldest dregs. Everyone ate with their fingers and wiped them on the ground or on their clothing.

Common foods eaten in **Mongolia** at the time:

- Meat dumplings
- Mutton
- Goat
- Beef jerky
- Yogurt
- Camel milk
- Kefir
- Onions and garlic
- Cabbage
- Carrots
- Potatoes
- Cheese

Cooking up a Mongolian feast in the 1500s

MONGOLIAN
Kitchen Tools

MONGOLS WEREN'T BIG ON TOOLS. THEY HAD TO CARRY EVERYTHING WITH THEM AS THEY TRAVELED, SO LESS WAS MORE. SOME ITEMS THEY DID USE IN THEIR MOBILE CAMPING KITCHENS INCLUDED:

Cast-Iron Pans and Pots

These were popular cooking vessels.

CAST-IRON PAN

Portable Stoves

Meat was boiled more often than it was roasted, and skewers were used for stirring and serving.

Animal-Skin Bags

Food was cooked in animal-skin pouches, and kefir and yogurt were fermented in animal stomachs. The stomachs were filled with milk and then hung in the gers' doorways so that people could knock the milk around and keep it mixing constantly.

MENUS OF THE
Rich & Famished

In 1420, a Persian historian traveled along China's portion of the Silk Road and recorded his journey. He and his companions were celebrated with feasts at every stop by local Chinese officials. At one dinner inside a canvas tent on a high hill, meat, geese, fowl, and dried and fresh fruit were served on "China dishes"—what we now simply call china. They were sent on their way with sheep, flour, and barley as gifts.

Wealthy Mongols, those who had the most possessions or were part of the largest tribes, would host a barbecue feast called a *khorkhog*. Guests watched as someone filled an emptied goat's stomach with hot rocks; chopped mutton; vegetables like carrots, cabbage, and potatoes; and water. The hot stones cooked the contents inside the stomach. If there weren't many animals to eat, horses were sometimes served for a big feast. Wealthier guests carried knives and spoons, some of which had been made from tree roots, on their belts to these parties.

SUGAR = GOLD

Sugar was a prized item traded on the Silk Road, although it had been around for thousands of years. Sugarcane was first cultivated in New Guinea, but sugar was first manufactured in India. When Persia's Emperor Darius invaded India in 510 B.C., he reported that there was a "reed which gives honey without bees." The Arabs and crusaders were next to discover sugar, and it could be found in England by 1099. In 1319, sugar sold for about $100 per kilogram, or 2.2 pounds, making it a real luxury. No wonder Silk Road traders were sweet on it.

YUCKY
HABITS
OF YORE

In the 1230s, the Mongols built a fountain that spouted fermented mares' milk.

Mongol soldiers might drink their horses' blood or milk if they were thirsty.

The Mongols believed animals had to be killed in the shadows so the sun wouldn't see it happen. They didn't want the earth to know about the sacrifice either, so they made sure not to spill blood on the ground.

By the Numbers

2 YEARS: How long it would have taken to travel from Rome to Beijing by horseback on the Silk Road. (Today you can fly from Rome to Beijing in 10 hours!)

1.2 MILLION: The population of Baghdad, Iraq, the largest city on the Silk Road from A.D. 1000 to 1300.

Some of the more unusual items traded on the Silk Road included lions, tigers, and camels; exotic fruits such as watermelons, peaches, grapes, and melons; and umbrellas and paper, which the Chinese invented and perfected.

Eat THIS

BUUZ OFF DUMPLINGS WITH SILK ROAD SAUCE

Buuz is Mongolian for dumplings. These are fun to make but take a bit of time. For that reason, make double what you want now and freeze the rest for the next time you have a dumpling craving. You can use any kind of ground meat, or go vegetarian and use 12 ounces (340 g) of firm tofu instead.

Makes 4 Servings

1 tablespoon (15 ml) olive oil

1 tablespoon (15 ml) sesame oil

1/2 pound (250 g) green vegetables, such as cabbage or bok choy, finely chopped

1/2 onion, peeled and minced

1/2 pound (225 g) ground pork

1 tablespoon (15 ml) low-sodium soy sauce

1 egg

1 package (48 count) 3-inch dumpling or wonton wrappers

Dipping Sauce (optional): 2 tablespoons (30 ml) low-sodium soy sauce, 1 teaspoon (5 ml) honey, 1/2 teaspoon (2.5 ml) sesame oil, and grated fresh ginger or 1/4 teaspoon (60 mg) dried ginger

1 Ask an adult to warm the olive and sesame oils in a large sauté pan over medium heat. Add the green vegetables and onion and cook for 3 minutes. Add the pork and stir, breaking up the meat, and then cook for about 6 minutes. Add the soy sauce and stir for 2 minutes more. Ask an adult to drain any excess liquid from the pan.

2 Meanwhile, fill a large stockpot with water and ask an adult to bring it to a boil over medium-high heat. In a small bowl, combine the egg with 2 tablespoons water and mix well.

3 Assemble the dumplings: Dip your finger in the egg water and wet the edges of each dumpling wrapper. Place about 1 heaping teaspoon of the filling in the middle of each wrapper and fold the circle in half (or fold the square in half). With your fingers or a fork's tines, pinch the wrapper together to seal completely so the filling won't leak. Pinch the ends together to make an Asian dumpling shape. Repeat with the remaining filling and wrappers.

4 Ask an adult to carefully add the dumplings in batches of about 5 to the water once it has boiled and cook for 2 to 3 minutes. Use a colander or slotted spoon to remove and place on a plate. Serve with dipping sauce or any sauce you like.

> " Rockin' delicious! I like that I can pop the whole thing in my mouth! "
> Indiana, 11

YURT-GURT

Back on the Silk Road, kids might have eaten even more yogurt than they do now. Nomads milked their goats or whatever animal they were shepherding and made yogurt by letting the milk ferment for days in a warm place. While it's super easy to grab a delicious non-sugary yogurt at the store, it's also super easy to make it at home. Try this foolproof method—you only need some jars and an ovenproof thermometer. We added vanilla to this yogurt, but if you want to make plain, just skip the vanilla.

Makes 4 Servings

1/2 gallon (1.9 L) whole milk

2 tablespoons (30 ml) pure vanilla extract (or 2 vanilla beans, split)

1 tablespoon (15 ml) honey

1/2 cup (120 ml) plain yogurt

Equipment: 4 pint-size canning jars

1 If you have mason or canning jars and a dishwasher, wash the jars in the dishwasher and let dry. If you don't have a dishwasher, sterilize the jars the old-fashioned way: Fill a large stainless steel pot with water, submerge the jars, and ask an adult to turn the heat to medium high and boil for 10 minutes. Ask an adult to move the pot, still covered, off the heat. When you're ready to use the jars, drain them.

2 Add milk to a large heavy-bottom stockpot. Whisk in the vanilla extract or scrape the vanilla beans into the milk. Add the honey and combine thoroughly.

3 Ask an adult to help you warm the milk mixture over medium heat until it reaches 190°F/88°C, and then take the pan off the heat. Let the milk cool on its own to 120°F/49°C.

4 Whisk in the yogurt until it's incorporated. Ask an adult to help you pour the milk into jars (you can use a funnel if you're worried about spilling) and seal with lids.

5 Place them in a cooler and pour warm water (about 120°F/49°C) into the cooler so that it comes about 3/4 of the way up the containers and leave for 3 hours. Or do like they did on the Silk Road and leave the yogurts in a warm spot covered with a dish towel for at least 6 hours or overnight.

6 Place in the refrigerator to cool and set for at least 3 hours or overnight. Eat. Yum!

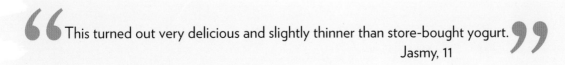

" This turned out very delicious and slightly thinner than store-bought yogurt. "
Jasmy, 11

POP CORNY quiz

1 How do scientists know there was early Silk Road trading going on thousands of years ago?

A. They read it in a book.
B. Their moms told them.
C. They found Egyptian mummies buried with Chinese silk.
D. Their dogs said so.
E. They dreamed it.

3 What was usually used to start a fire on the Silk Road?

A. Dried hippo nails
B. Dried gers
C. Dried paper
D. Dried animal poop
E. Dried flowers

2 How often were a Mongol's caftans washed?

A. Twice a day
B. Twice a year
C. Once in their lifetime
D. On their birthday each year
E. Never

4 At what age did Mongol boys become soldiers?

A. 3   D. 23
B. 5   E. 104
C. 15

5

What is kefir?

A. Fermented milk
B. Fermented mouse breath
C. Fermented cheese
D. Fermented sand
E. Fermented dragon

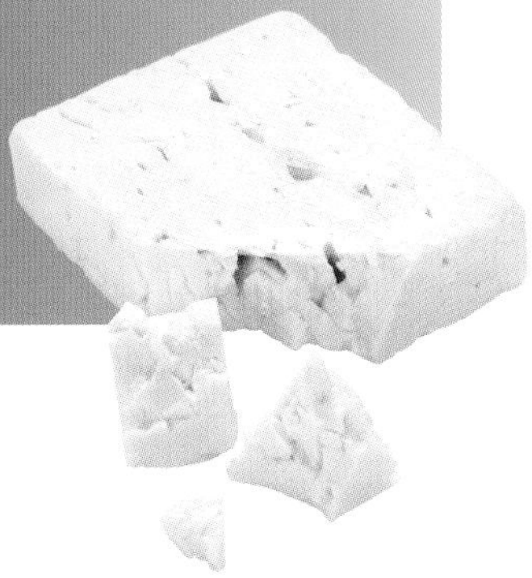

6

What city now stands in Kublai Khan's old capital?

A. Laos
B. Tokyo
C. Xian
D. Seoul
E. Beijing

Mongol men often rode with a **small animal-skin pouch** containing meat, wild onions, and rice under their saddles. By day's end, the heat of the horse, the saddle, and the rider would have **warmed the food.**

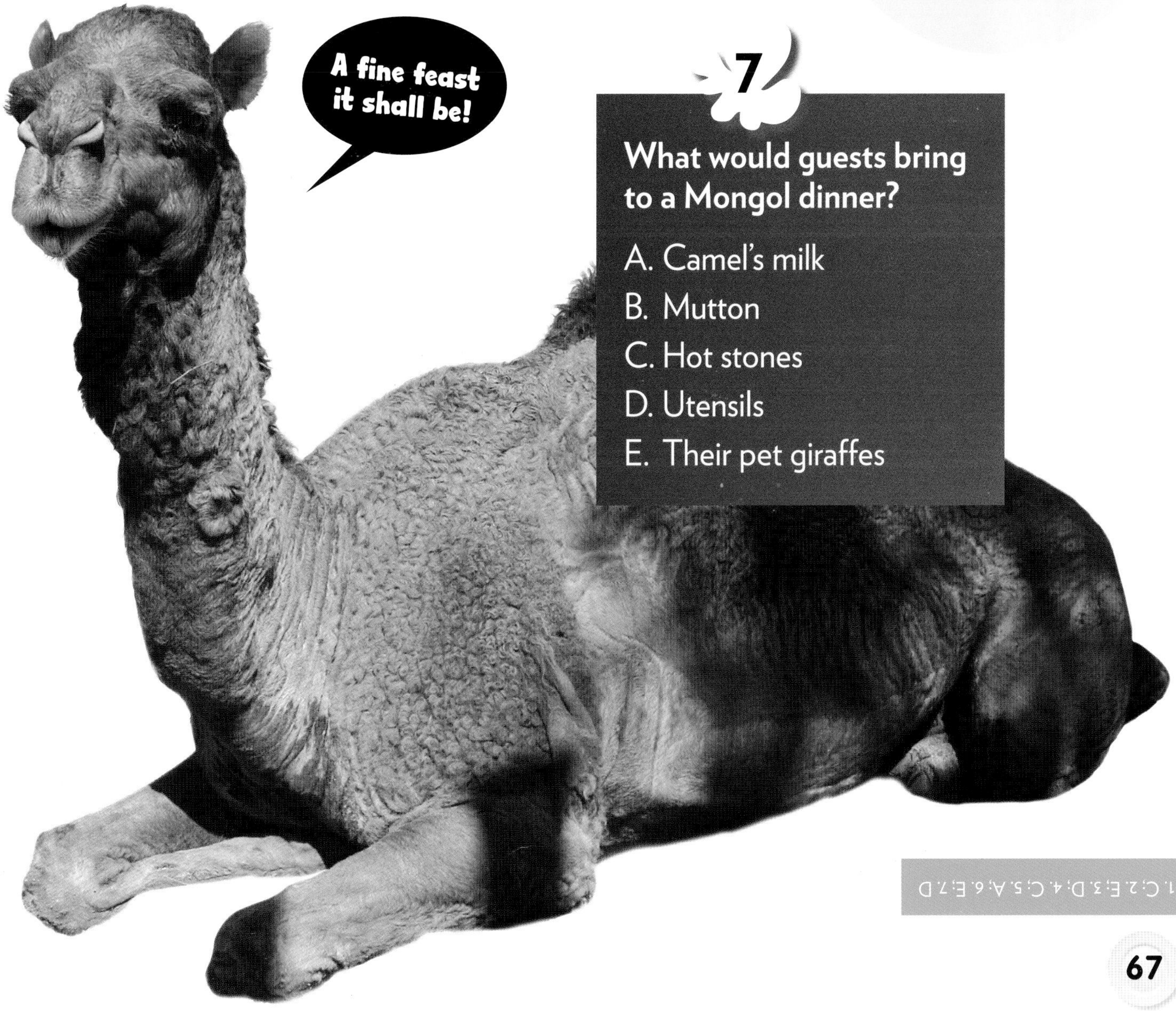

A fine feast it shall be!

7

What would guests bring to a Mongol dinner?

A. Camel's milk
B. Mutton
C. Hot stones
D. Utensils
E. Their pet giraffes

Answers: 1. C; 2. E; 3. D; 4. C; 5. A; 6. E; 7. D

The Renaissance:
Turnspit Dogs, Sugar Castles, and Flying Machines

A BITE-SIZE history

Lifelike art, memorable plays, futuristic inventions—these were hallmarks of the Renaissance. Literally meaning "rebirth," the Renaissance was a period, from the 14th to the 17th century, when the world enjoyed renewed creativity, invention, and a focus on learning.

In the 14th century, the economy of Europe began to flourish, and there was an uptick in the trading and selling of goods between Europe, the Mediterranean, and Asia. This resulted in the growth of the middle class as more people opened small businesses to produce or sell goods and services. That, in turn, led to more people having more money to spend on everything from spices to pots to furs.

Italy, conveniently located between the Mediterranean Sea and the rest of Europe, especially reaped the benefits of all this trade, and it developed a booming economy for the middle and upper classes. Florence, an Italian city midway between Rome and Milan, became one of the most important cities in the world for trading not just goods but also ideas.

During the Renaissance, people began to consider new ways to paint, build, write, and even think. In 1495, an Italian named Leonardo da Vinci started painting "The Last Supper," depicting Jesus surrounded by his followers at his final dinner before his death. Nearly a decade later, Leonardo took paintbrush to canvas to create the "Mona Lisa," a woman with a mysterious smile. These paintings, with their accurate details of both the human body and human expressions, captured the people and places, heroes and heroines of the time. Today, enthralled crowds wait in line for hours to see them in museums and cathedrals because they are considered masterpieces of the

Present-day boundaries are shown.

Milan

Florence

ITALY

Rome

JOHANNES GUTENBERG SHOWS A PAGE FROM HIS PRINTED BIBLE.

Renaissance. Leonardo, who was celebrated as a great artist and thinker during his life, was so ahead of his time that he imagined a day when tanks and parachutes would be invented. And most amazingly, he thought that the carts he saw on Florence's streets would one day be replaced by flying machines. He drew diagrams of these machines, which resemble what Orville and Wilbur Wright created 400 years later when they built the world's first airplane.

Another Italian artist, Michelangelo Buonarroti, chiseled a mammoth block of marble into an enormous statue of a perfect man named David. Michelangelo went on to spend the next several years on his back on a scaffolding, painting figures from the Bible on the very high and very large ceiling of the Vatican's Sistine Chapel in Rome. Like Leonardo, Michelangelo became a renowned artist of the Renaissance, famous in his lifetime and to this day for his beautiful and realistic representations of people and places.

There were also major advancements in communication: Johannes Gutenberg of Germany invented an easily usable movable type and printing press. For the first time, books could be printed quickly rather than being handwritten or block printed with ink. This might not seem like a big deal today, but the printing press changed the course of the world!

MICHEL-
ANGELO'S
"DAVID"
IS 14 FEET
(4.3 M) TALL!

Why? Creating multiple copies of books became simple and made them more affordable. That meant more people were able to buy them, so more people learned to read. For the first time, books were crossing into other cultures. Language, math, and knowledge began to spread across vast lands.

And what books did people read back then? Perhaps Gutenberg's printed version of the Bible, now known as the Gutenberg Bible (21 complete copies of it still exist today). Or maybe it was the beautifully written and timeless plays by up-and-coming actor William Shakespeare. (Some theatergoers didn't think they were all wonderful and apparently threw rotten fruits and nuts at the actors to express their irritation.) All 37 are still performed around the world today, but we don't throw fruits and nuts anymore.

Or perhaps they were reading copies of the 95 Theses, an angry letter that a German named Martin Luther wrote and nailed to the door of a Catholic Church. Luther was protesting certain church practices and abuses; his objections and recommendations helped begin a new religion called Protestantism.

People also read about food! Cookbooks started to be published and printed during the Renaissance, which meant that recipes for sauces, cakes, roasts, and more began to spread around the world.

Women wore makeup made from **dried egg** whites to make their faces as pale as possible.

> If you want to be healthy **observe this regime.** Do not eat when you have no appetite and dine lightly, **chew well**, and whatever you take into you should be **well-cooked** and of **simple ingredients.**

Artist and inventor Leonardo da Vinci, 1515

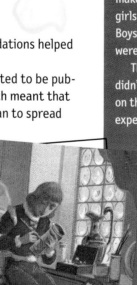

A YOUNG ARTIST

A DAY
in the Life:
Florence, 1522

Buongiorno! Many children in Florence may have woken up on straw-stuffed mattresses and peeked out the window of their little brick home on an Italian hillside to greet the day.

Time to get dressed! Girls had to be really ready for this process because it took *forever*. They had to put on an underdress, stockings, a corset, a bodice, petticoats, a heavier dress on top of it all, and a headdress to cover their hair. Even on hot summer days! Boys got off easier, wearing jackets with shorts or breeches and tights. Moms or *nonnas* (Italian for "grandmothers") usually made breakfast, which was probably cold leftovers from the previous night or a cold mush of oats and some veggies or scraps of meat.

In the 1500s, more than half of Europe's population had just barely enough money and food to survive. Six days a week (Sunday was a rest day), parents and kids worked. Children spent a lot of their day learning the skills they would be using as adults. Girls practiced sewing and cooking. Boys focused on their future jobs, such as being, say, a baker, butcher, or candlestick maker. Only boys from wealthy families went to school. When girls turned 14, they were legally adults and allowed to marry. Boys weren't considered adults until they were 21; however, they were often sent off to work or apprentice as young as seven.

The poorest families ate only one meal a day because they didn't have the money to buy much food. It changed depending on the season, but meat was rarely on the menu because it was expensive. Typical foods were rye and barley bread with some hard cheese. Rich families had multiple meals with dozens of courses that included lamb chops with rosemary, roast venison with cloves, and marzipan in the shape of flowers. That's why being plump was a sign of nobility—it meant you had enough money to eat all the food you desired.

If there was any free time in the day, children might play conkers, a game that involved hanging horse chestnuts (conkers) on strings and hitting their opponent's conkers, or they'd play tag or fetch with the dog.

After the day's last meal or snack, it would be *buona notte* (good night). Everyone scrambled back into their linen or woolen nightgowns and nightcaps and thought about all of the things there were to paint, build, and cook tomorrow.

Spicing Things Up!

During the Renaissance, people continued to fish, hunt, and farm their food just as they had for thousands of years. While preserved food was popular, some people thought fresh fruits and vegetables could be poisonous. Even though families still grew and prepared almost everything they ate, from bacon and bread to honey and pickled fruits and veggies, a huge portion of their income was spent on food. They went to markets to buy ingredients they couldn't make at home.

The most expensive and sought-after ingredients at the time weren't meat or candy. They were spices. Before modern refrigerators and freezers, spices and salt played an even bigger role in cooking than they do today. Seasonings made two-week-old meat taste better, and salt helped make food last longer. Spices even doubled as medicine. In fact, spices were kept under lock and key in many homes. Sailors who brought spices back to their countries made a lot of money. Importing even a small amount of nutmeg could earn them enough to buy a house. Imagine how much could be bought with the jar of ground nutmeg in your kitchen!

Most uninsulated kitchens of the times were cool in winter and hot in summer. Chilly basement rooms called larders were used for drying or salting meat, which preserved them for months. Food was cooked in a fireplace, either on spits (long iron rods hung over a fire) or boiled in large cast-iron cauldrons. Brick ovens were used to bake bread and other goods, such as fruit pies.

Burnt mint and rosemary, as well as other herbs, were used as **toothpaste.**

Table matters!

The one full meal most people ate each day was dinner, served at midday. A lighter meal, supper, was eaten in the early evening. All dishes were served at the same time on big platters. In wealthier homes, everyone was expected to leave some leftover food, called manners, for the servants.

In poorer homes, wooden dishes were used, while the wealthy had gold or silver plates. Knives and spoons were fairly common; forks were mainly used for serving food. Some people did use forks to eat pasta, an uncommon treat at the time because it had to be made fresh, which was a lot of work. Diners shared plates and cups, so it was important to wipe mouths and fingers with napkins before taking bites and sips.

Most families sat at wooden tables with long benches. Chairs were used only by the wealthy. Often the dining room had large cupboards for storing food and a prized pot and pan (few people had more than one of each).

Common foods eaten during the Renaissance:

- Ox
- Wild boar
- Peacock
- Sturgeon
- Pork
- Lamb
- Stew
- Polenta
- Sugar
- Honey
- Pickled vegetables
- Hard and soft cheeses
- Olives
- Stewed fruits
- Bread

A
*Renaissance
family feast*

RENAISSANCE
Kitchen Tools

KITCHEN TOOLS WERE BECOMING MORE DECORATIVE AND EASIER TO USE. SOME OF THE MOST POPULAR STATE-OF-THE-ART ITEMS INCLUDED:

Turnspit Dog

Starting in the 16th century, this small pooch, also known as the cooking dog, kitchen dog, or underdog, was trained to run in a wheel that turned a spit in front of a fire to evenly roast meat.

A CHALICE BEFITTING ROYALTY

Gorgeous Goblets

Real glass encrusted with expensive gems was a favorite at royal courts around Europe.

Pasta Cutters

Even though pasta wasn't eaten as often as it is today, small serrated cutters were invented to make different sizes and shapes of pasta, such as ravioli, linguine, and lasagna noodles.

Pastry Cutters

Cookie cutters in shapes like hearts, diamonds, and crescent moons were popular.

During childbirth, women were given oil and vinegar to drink, and **eagle poop** was used as a balm to relieve pain.

Water was often stored in tanks lined with **lead**, which poisoned the water and anyone who drank it.

Some believed the **bubonic plague** could be cured by snuggling up with a live hen and **drinking urine**!

MENUS OF THE
Rich & Famished

For the wealthy, it wasn't a party unless enormous amounts of meat and crazy sugar creations were served. Big centerpieces, like a roasted whole head of wild boar with a lemon in its mouth and ivy wrapped around its ears, were served at many banquets.

Some royal households served mini castles made of the increasingly popular ingredient known as sugar to show off how much money they had. But sugar sculptures fell out of favor when a new cold treat became all the rage: ice cream. The chilly food made its way around Europe's royal courts in the late 1600s and became a craze after England's King Charles II featured orange blossom ice cream at one of his parties. It was such a big hit that he paid the ice-cream cook a salary just to keep the recipe a secret!

By the **Numbers**
2,800: The number of plates
used at a dinner given by Alfonso d'Este, the Duke of Ferrara, in 1529, for 104 guests. That's 27 plates per person!

FOWL MOST FOUL

A banquet held in Rome in 1473 would have impressed even their Roman ancestors with its lavishness. Bernardino Corio, a historian of the time, recorded that trays made of real silver and gold held "pork livers, blancmange, meats with relish, tortes and pies, salt-cured pork loin and sausage, roast veal, kid [baby goat], squab, chicken, rabbit … whole roasted large game, and fowl dressed in their skin or feathers. Next came golden tortes and muscat pears in cups." And that was just the first course!

The Medici family, Florence's richest and noblest family, kept **lions** and **giraffes** in one of the city's main squares. Sometimes the giraffes **escaped** and could be found peeking into windows in the city's streets.

Eat THIS

THE APPLE OF SHAKESPEARE'S EYE

"Quarter them, and lay them betweene two sheetes of Paste: put in a piece of whole Sinamon, two or three bruised Cloues, a little sliced Ginger, Orrengado, or onely the yellow outside of the Orenge, a bit of sweet Butter about the bignesse of an Egge, good store of Sugar: sprinckle on a little Rosewater. Then close your Tart, and bake it."

This recipe is based on the above, which is known as "A Quarter Tart of Pippins" from *A New Booke of Cookerie* by John Murrell, 1615. While phyllo dough wasn't used in Europe, it was in the Mediterranean. We chose it because it's light and healthy, but you can also put the apple filling in a regular piecrust.

Makes 8 Servings

5 Golden Delicious apples—peeled, cored, and thinly sliced

1 teaspoon (2.3 g) cinnamon

1/2 teaspoon (2.5 g) ground ginger

1 tablespoon (15 ml) honey

2 tablespoons (30 ml) melted butter, plus more cold butter for greasing

1/2 cup (75 g) raisins or dried cranberries or dried cherries

2 tablespoons (28 g) grated orange or lemon zest

1/2 package frozen phyllo dough, defrosted

1 Ask an adult to preheat the oven to 375°F/190°C. In a large bowl, combine the apples, cinnamon, ginger, honey, 1 tablespoon of melted butter, raisins, and zest.

2 Grease a large pie pan with some cold butter. Gently pull out four sheets of phyllo and place into the pie dish in the shape of an X, overlaying one on top of the other. Working quickly (phyllo gets more delicate to work with the warmer it becomes), with a pastry brush or spoon gently coat the phyllo with a little melted butter.

3 Add two more layers, one across the other, and brush with a little bit of butter. Add the apple mixture. Add two more layers of phyllo on top in an X shape, then fold the phyllo over, tucking it all around and in to make the outer crust rim. Brush the last of the butter on top, and ask an adult to transfer it to the oven. Bake until the apples are tender and the phyllo is golden brown, about 45 minutes.

"There's no drama with this tart. The light flakiness of the phyllo dough mixes beautifully with the Golden Delicious apples to create an overall scrumptious experience."
Mary, 14

UNCRUEL GRUEL

Gruel can be made of almost anything—rice, oats, wheat or rye flour—and was a staple food for thousands of years throughout the world. We like this version from Hannah Woolley, who wrote *Rich Cabinet: Scored with All Manner of Rare Receipts for Preserving, Candying or Cookery* in 1672. She explains: "To make a Rice pudding to bake. Take three Pints of Milk or more, and put therein a quarter of a Pound of Rice, clean washed and picked, then set them over the fire, and let them warm together, and often stir them with a wooden Spoon." To make it healthier, we substituted brown rice for the usual white.

Makes 6 Servings

2-1/2 cups (591 ml) water

1 cup (190 g) long-grain brown rice (or short-grain, 200 g)

3 cups (720 ml) milk or Almond Milk for Lords and Ladies (page 54)

2 tablespoons (30 ml) honey

1 teaspoon (2.3 g) cinnamon or nutmeg

1 teaspoon (5 ml) vanilla extract

3/4 cup (115 g) raisins or dried cranberries

1/2 teaspoon (2.5 g) salt

1 Ask an adult to bring the water to a boil over medium-high heat in a large stockpot, and then add the rice. Ask an adult to reduce the heat to low and cover. Simmer for about 40 minutes or until the rice is tender.

2 Add the milk, honey, cinnamon, vanilla, raisins or dried cranberries, and salt and stir to combine. Heat for about 4 minutes, stirring often. Serve warm or cold.

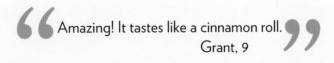

"Amazing! It tastes like a cinnamon roll."
Grant, 9

POP CORNY quiz

1 How many plates per person were served at the Duke of Ferrara's banquet?

A. 27
B. 42
C. 2
D. 1,089
E. 780,056,033,363,292

2 What was the one ingredient not served in Italy during this time?

A. Bird droppings
B. Olives
C. Mozzarella
D. Sturgeon
E. Sugar

3 What was likely thrown at actors by unhappy theatergoers at Shakespeare's plays?

A. Coconuts and lemons
B. Avocados and pineapples
C. Rotten fruit and nuts
D. Porcupines and pheasants
E. Bows and arrows

4 What popular dish was served in Europe's royal courts?

A. Eye of newt
B. Beak of bee
C. Brain of snail
D. Ice cream
E. Ear of mouse

Say what!?

5

The fork was used mostly for what?

A. As a mini sword
B. To dig up veggies
C. Pointing to lessons on a
   chalkboard
D. Serving food and eating pasta
E. As soap

$$c^2 = a^2 + b^2$$
$$c = \sqrt{a^2 + b^2}$$
$$a = \sqrt{c^2 - b^2}$$
$$b = \sqrt{c^2 - a^2}$$

6

At what age were boys considered adults?

A. 3
B. 7
C. 21
D. 47
E. 106

7

What did some people use for toothpaste?

A. Guacamole
B. Mint and rosemary
C. Snail slime
D. Potatoes
E. Strawberry juice

America
Revolts:
Iced Tea, False Teeth, and Flummeries and Syllabubs

A BITE-SIZE
history

While Europe was still in the afterglow of the Renaissance's brilliance, over in the New World, which included North America, life wasn't quite as easy. And after a "shot heard round the world," nothing would ever be the same.

Beginning in the late 1500s, people from Great Britain started coming "across the pond," as the saying goes, crossing the Atlantic Ocean to seek freedom, religious liberty, and a way to make—not gain—a few pounds (British money was used initially in the New World's early British settlements). One hundred four adventuresome Brits founded a little village in 1607 in Jamestown, Virginia, creating a permanent settlement; in 1620 a jam-packed ship called the *Mayflower* set sail for Virginia with 102 people—some of whom were Puritans—along with some sheep, dogs, and goats. But they landed instead on the rocky coast of what's now called Plymouth, Massachusetts.

In the following decades, the settlements grew and more people joined the Native American tribes that had been there for at least 13,000 years. Many native peoples were killed or faced great suffering because of European settlers.

Gradually, 13 colonies formed, from New Hampshire all the way down to Georgia, but they were all still governed by Great Britain. By 1770, more than two million people lived in these colonies, and about 20 percent of those were slaves violently brought to the New World against their will from Africa.

Long-distance governing grew increasingly difficult for Great Britain's King George III. He wanted more control over, and money from, the Colonies. So Parliament (Britain's governing body) started raising taxes on their everyday items,

GEORGE WASHINGTON RODE THE U.S. TO VICTORY.

CANADA

UNITED STATES

Lexington
Concord
Philadelphia
Jamestown
Boston
Plymouth
New York
Yorktown

such as sugar. In Great Britain, citizens couldn't be taxed without their parliamentary representatives agreeing to it, but the colonists didn't have anyone representing them.

A tax called the Stamp Act of 1765 angered colonists so much that they refused to pay the taxes, declaring "no taxation without representation." The act was repealed four months later with the help of a Philadelphia diplomat wearing bifocals of his own invention. His name? Benjamin Franklin.

Anger continued to grow on both sides of the Atlantic, especially in March 1770, when five protestors were killed by British soldiers in what came to be called the Boston Massacre. Protests also brewed (get it?) after a tea tax was imposed in 1773, making it more expensive for colonists to drink their beloved tea.

On December 16, 1773, the Sons of Liberty, a group of colonial patriots, quietly snuck onto three ships in Boston's harbor to throw all of the ships' 342 tea chests into the icy waters to protest the tea tax. Some of them were disguised as Native Americans. It seems the tax was not their cup of tea either.

The British Parliament retaliated against what became known as the Boston Tea Party by taking away Massachusetts's few self-governing rules and closing Boston's port. The Colonies decided it was time to unite and fight back. In 1774, representatives from 12 of the 13

Colonies (Georgia opted out) attended the First Continental Congress in Philadelphia, Pennsylvania. Delegates John Adams, Patrick Henry, Samuel Adams, and others wrote a petition to King George stating they wanted a repeal of all parliamentary acts and taxes on the Colonies, that Parliament had no right to be in charge of local issues, and that having British troops stationed in the Colonies was against the law.

In response, Britain declared that Massachusetts was in rebellion on February 9, 1775, and sent 2,000 more British soldiers to protect its New World lands.

On April 19, 1775, battles were fought in Lexington and Concord, beginning with a "shot heard round the world," as writer Ralph Waldo Emerson called it. The American Revolution had officially begun.

Weeks later in Philadelphia, the Second Continental Congress met and appointed a tall congressman from Virginia as commander in chief of the new Continental Army. This 43-year-old former solider, George Washington, with white powdered hair and fake teeth made of ivory, took charge.

> **Vegetables …** constitute my principal diet.
>
> **Thomas Jefferson, who lived to the then very old age of 83**

While the soldiers fought, the Continental Congress decided to form its own nation. On July 4, 1776, the Declaration of Independence, written by Thomas Jefferson and edited by the Congress, was signed. It stated that the Colonies would no longer be under British rule and would form a new nation, the United States of America. This now famous sentence appears in this announcement to the world: "We hold these truths to be self-evident, that all men are created equal, that they are endowed by their Creator with certain unalienable Rights, that among these are Life, Liberty and the pursuit of Happiness." France eventually came to America's aid, having recognized the independent nation in 1777.

By the summer of 1781, both sides were enduring terrible conditions, including starvation, lack of medical care for injured soldiers, and diminishing weapons supplies. Yet the American and French armies headed to Yorktown, Virginia, for what turned out to be the final battle. On October 17, 1781, the British surrendered after 7,000 of their soldiers had been captured.

The brutal eight-year American Revolution resulted in horrific losses, but it also gave birth to a new independent nation. In 1787, the Continental Congress met in Philadelphia to create a formal government that was divided into three branches—judicial, legislative, and executive, thus ensuring that no branch would have too much power. The document they wrote detailing how their government worked was the Constitution.

So what did citizens of this new country love to eat?

THE BOSTON TEA PARTY HEATS UP

A DAY in the Life: Boston, 1781

Children growing up in this bustling New England city might wake up in little brick homes in narrow beds, splash some cold water on their faces, and change out of their nightshirts. Boys threw on a shirt, short jacket, and long pants or knee britches. Girls put on long loose floral dresses. They'd have some bread and milk for breakfast with their family in a small dining room before heading to school, work, or to help their parents.

Boys who apprenticed with, say, a baker would get the oven fired up, feed the horses, load the bread onto the wagon, and deliver the big round loaves to homes. Girls who stayed home to assist their mothers would gather and prepare the food for the day's meals, repair torn clothes, or sweep out the dust kicked up by the endless stream of horses that rode past their windows. Kids in the middle class were allowed to attend school for free to learn how to read and write; those in wealthy families in the mid-Atlantic and South had tutors. Enslaved children were usually not taught at all. In fact, it was illegal in many states to teach slaves to read.

However they spent their mornings, children would probably come back from chores, an apprenticeship, or school to eat dinner, which was served in early afternoon. Pemmican was a typical snack: Made from dried meat and berries pounded together, this Native American staple was the first energy bar, providing a boost to play nine pins (similar to bowling), roll hoops, do puzzles, or spin wool into yarn.

What was for nightly supper? Often leftovers.

Days rarely ended with a nice warm bath because the water would have to be drawn by hand from the public well—there was no running water yet—so it would need to be heated in the fireplace before being poured into a tin tub, which was usually placed in the warm kitchen. So most nights, kids would splash some water on their faces and head to bed, dreaming of what the future held now that they weren't long-distance British citizens.

A FAVORITE COLONIAL KIDS GAME

Spicing Things Up!

Before the Revolution, the Colonies depended on the British Empire's trade companies for luxuries like tea and spices. But once they were independent, they had to find a way to generate all their own food and to acquire trade goods for themselves.

Native Americans were skilled hunters and farmers; they taught some colonists their best methods and how to use local staples like corn, squash, and beans.

Other popular foods arrived in the New World with African slaves, including okra, watermelon, black-eyed peas, rice, peanuts, and yams. Many dishes that are considered southern fare today have African culinary roots.

While the Colonies had some of the most amazing fruits and vegetables growing anywhere, most people only ate them cooked, thinking raw produce wasn't very tasty. They also used age-old methods of preserving foods like smoking, drying, pickling, and salting.

Those who lived in big cities headed to what we now call a farmers market to buy produce, meats, and fish in a public square. Foods like rice, fish, and beef were also shipped between colonies, so a person in Boston could eat, say, South Carolina rice. Bakeries were popular because many people didn't have the time or ovens to make their own bread.

Common foods eaten at the time:

- Maize (corn)
- Clams
- Cranberries
- Potatoes
- Cod
- Oysters
- Yams
- Squirrel
- Beaver
- Otter
- Porcupine
- Seal
- Pig
- Fruit pies
- Fruits and veggies
- Bread
- Turkey
- Beef

Table matters!

Do you sit at the kids' table at Thanksgiving? That's a British custom brought over by colonists. But in some homes during the colonial era, kids weren't allowed to sit at all. Instead they stood at the table or even behind their parents' seats, waiting to be handed food.

In the southern colonies, which retained Britain's more formal customs and etiquette, kids had to follow rules similar to those in the 16th-century book *The Schole of Vertue:* "Never sit down at the table till asked, and after the blessing. Ask for nothing; tarry till it be offered thee. Speak not. Bite not thy bread but break it. Take salt only with a clean knife. Dip not the meat in the same. Hold not thy knife upright but sloping, and lay it down at right hand of plate with blade on plate. Look not earnestly at any other that is eating. When moderately satisfied leave the table. Sing not, hum not, wriggle not. Spit no where in the room but in the corner." Hmm ... quite different from today!

Many people didn't have glasses to drink from, as glass wouldn't be widely available until the 1800s. But they did have wooden or tin plates and bowls, earthenware cups, and knives. Forks and spoons were rare. Many ate with their hands.

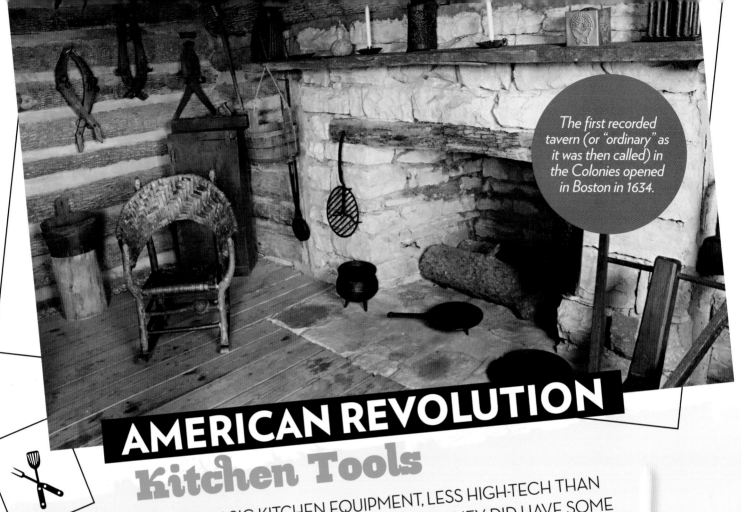

AMERICAN REVOLUTION

Kitchen Tools

THE COLONIES HAD BASIC KITCHEN EQUIPMENT, LESS HIGH-TECH THAN WHAT WAS COMMON IN EUROPE AT THE TIME. BUT THEY DID HAVE SOME ESSENTIAL ITEMS TO CHURN OUT YUMMY FOODS:

Beehive Ovens

Situated next to the fireplace and shaped like a beehive, these were used for baking breads, pies, and cakes.

Bake Kettles

Large deep pots made of brass, copper, or iron were used to cook everything; they were so treasured that they were passed down through generations and included in wills. One of the most favored types of kettle was the lidded cast-iron bake kettle pot.

Spit Jack

A hand-cranked rod used for turning meat over a fire.

Candles

Each household made their own candles (the average house needed 400 a year) from smoky, smelly animal fat, very expensive beeswax, or spermaceti from whales, which produced a brighter, less smoky candle and was often used in kitchens.

Ice

Wealthy homes packed their basements with enormous blocks of ice that had been harvested in the North. The ice was wrapped in straw, and they stored foods on top of them. It was a colonial refrigerator!

Wooden Paddles

These were used to remove food from the beehive oven, similar to what some pizzerias use today.

Spider

A skillet with three short legs, which could be placed atop coals, embers, or wood to cook smaller portions of foods.

Running Water

Philadelphia homes got the first running water in 1801, followed by New York in 1842, Boston in 1848, and Chicago around 1865.

People used to relieve themselves in chamber pots while sitting right at the dining room table! Luckily, they were concealed by the tablecloth.

MENUS OF THE
Rich & Famished

Fancy dinner parties often featured turtle, as this Philadelphia family's menu shows from 1786: turtle soup, roast turkey and duck, veal and beef, two jelly desserts, plus puddings, pies, preserves, oranges, and apples.

At a 1774 Continental Congress meeting in Philadelphia, John Adams was served a late afternoon dinner that included not just turtle but many items unfamiliar to us today: "Turtle and every other thing, flummery, jellies, sweetmeats of 20 sorts, trifles, whipped syllabubs, floating islands, and fools."

Kids who went to lavish parties during the mid- to late-1700s might have had a taste of election cake, a beloved treat served in towns every Election Day in May. Often weighing in at 50 pounds (23 kg)—it had to feed the whole town—this yeasty sweet cake was always a big hit because of both its size and taste!

By the Numbers

2,000: Approximate number of plants Native Americans ate and used for cooking.

To increase the population of Georgia in 1735, its government offered a year's supply of food to any "working man" who moved there, including:

- **312 POUNDS** (141 kg) beef or pork
- **104 POUNDS** (47 kg) rice
- **104 POUNDS** (47 kg) Indian corn or peas
- **104 POUNDS** (47 kg) flour
- **24 POUNDS** (11 kg) salt
- **16 POUNDS** (7 kg) cheese
- **12 POUNDS** (5.5 kg) butter
- **12 POUNDS** (5.5 kg) sugar
- **4 GALLONS** (15 L) vinegar
- **8 OUNCES** (227 g) spices

Lobsters and oysters were so plentiful and cheap that they were considered food for the poor. Today, those two items are pretty expensive!

83

Eat THIS

AMELIA'S CHOUDER TO CHOW

This recipe is inspired by one for fish "chouder" from *American Cookery*, the first U.S. cookbook, written by Amelia Simmons in 1796. The modern version is packed with protein and heart-healthy omega-3s and is dee-lish-us! Serve with crusty toasty garlic-and-olive-oil bread or a trencher (page 55).

Makes 4 Servings

1 tablespoon (15 ml) olive oil

1 onion, peeled and chopped

3 red potatoes, cut into small chunks

1 cup (240 ml) low-sodium clam juice

1/2 teaspoon (2.5 g) salt

1/4 teaspoon (570 mg) freshly ground pepper

1/2 teaspoon (1 g) Old Bay seasoning or paprika

1 pound (454 g) cod fillet or other white fish such as haddock, bones and skin removed, cut into 2-inch pieces

4 cups (960 ml) water

1 cup (250 ml) sour cream or plain Greek yogurt

2 tablespoons (7.6 g) chopped fresh parsley, for topping (optional)

1 Ask an adult to warm the oil in a large nonstick stockpot over medium heat. Add the onion and sauté for 3 minutes. Add the potatoes, clam juice, salt, pepper, and Old Bay or paprika. Cook for 10 minutes.

2 Add the fish and 4 cups (960 ml) water. Cook, uncovered, for 20 minutes or until the potatoes are done. Stir in the sour cream and sprinkle with parsley, if using.

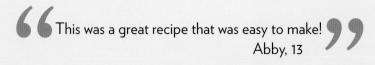

" This was a great recipe that was easy to make! "
Abby, 13

JOHNNY-ON-THE-SPOT CAKES

These cornmeal-like pancakes, also inspired by *American Cookery,* were extremely popular for breakfast and snacks during the colonial era. They're still perfect, especially when coated with nut butter and topped with the Lentil Stew for Junior Olympiads (page 34) or the Army's Non-Ghoulish Goulash (page 114). You can eat these as a tasty breakfast with a few berries on the side, or add sweet or savory toppings like maple syrup, honey, cheese, meat, or tomato sauce.

Makes 14 Cakes

1/2 cup (120 ml) water

2-1/2 cups (375 g) cornmeal

1/2 teaspoon (2.5 g) salt

4 tablespoons (60 ml) melted butter, plus 1 tablespoon (15 ml) cold butter

1 cup (240 ml) whole milk

1 egg

Maple syrup or honey, for serving

1 Ask an adult to help you boil the water. In a large bowl, mix the boiling water, cornmeal, salt, 4 tablespoons butter, milk, and egg. Stir well to combine.

2 Ask an adult to put the remaining tablespoon of butter into a large non-stick pan or a griddle and melt over medium heat. Add 2 tablespoons of batter into the pan for each cake and cook until golden brown underneath. Ask an adult to flip the cakes over and cook for another 3 minutes. Serve hot with maple syrup or honey.

> "When I eat these, I feel like I'm a Revolutionary War soldier holding a musket, ready to go to battle!"
> Josh, 12

POPCORNY quiz

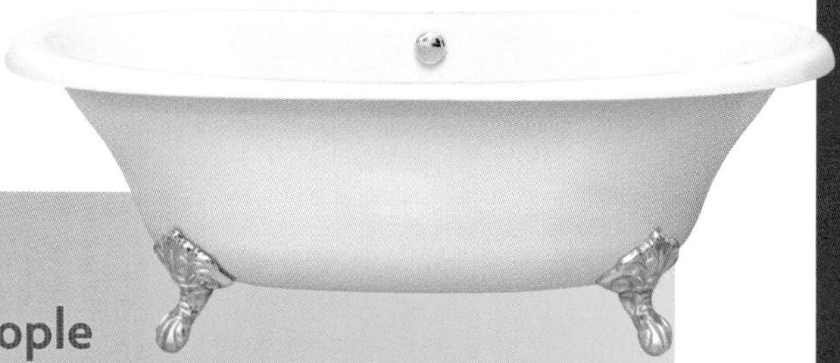

1

How did people take a bath in colonial times?

A. They turned on the bathtub's faucet.
B. They jumped into the shower.
C. They jumped in a horse's water trough.
D. They jumped in a portable tin tub in the kitchen.
E. They jumped onto a Slip 'N Slide.

2

How did Charleston's streets stay clean of food scraps?

A. An army of gerbils swept the streets.
B. Buzzards ate the scraps.
C. Garbage trucks drove around cleaning.
D. Vacuum robots cleaned the streets.
E. Kitties licked up the food.

3

Why was the beehive oven called that name?

A. It was shaped like a bee's beehive.
B. People ran around it like busy bees.
C. It was shaped like a woman's 1960s hairstyle.
D. Honey dripped out of it.
E. They ran out of names for ovens.

4

What was the first American cookbook called?

A. *Cookery American*
B. *Colonial American Cooks*
C. *American Cookery*
D. *American Cooks*
E. *Cook It Up America!*

Toe-tally gross!

5

Where, and when, did running water first appear in citizens' homes?

A. Philadelphia in 1801
B. New York in 1842
C. Boston in 1848
D. Chicago around 1865
E. All of the above

6

What did wealthy colonists use as a refrigerator?

A. The back of a cave
B. The inside of a bat's stomach
C. An igloo
D. The main cabin of an airplane
E. An ice-packed basement of a home

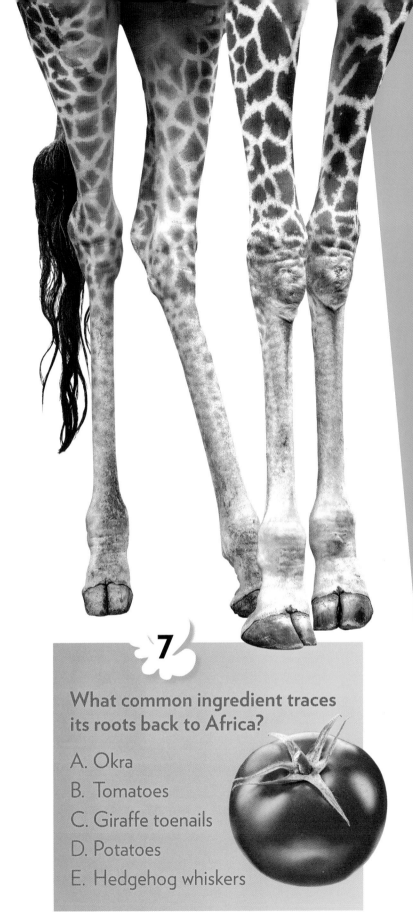

7

What common ingredient traces its roots back to Africa?

A. Okra
B. Tomatoes
C. Giraffe toenails
D. Potatoes
E. Hedgehog whiskers

The French
Revolution:
Terror Reigns, Restaurants Debut, and Few Eat Cake

A BITE-SIZE history

In 1778, King Louis XVI of France sent his army to help America's patriots fight the British, beginning a series of events that culminated in a revolution, a peasant uprising, and his head being chopped off. This violent time, beginning in 1789, ended the monarchy forever and turned not just France upside down but the entire world.

France was near bankruptcy in the 1780s, partly because of the help it provided to the Americans during the American Revolution and partly from the king's lavish spending. Poor harvests worsened the situation, resulting in food shortages and deaths from starvation. Yet hungry peasants, who made up 95 percent of the population, had to pay taxes while nobles didn't, keeping the poor poor and the rich rich. That was coupled with the fact that the peasants' staple food, bread, kept rising in price as production was reduced while the king stockpiled grain. This led to constant fears of famine and bread shortages, making the peasants angrier.

In 1787, the price of a loaf of bread had soared to what most peasants earned in a week, and the masses started to panic. The king, who lived in the gilded grand palace of Versailles, called a meeting to discuss how to deal with the crisis.

The Assembly of Notables, as the meeting was called, included three groups, or estates: the First Estate (Catholic clergy), the Second Estate (aristocrats), and the Third Estate (regular people). Things fell apart when the Third Estate called for a new governing body, the National Assembly, to represent them. The king, realizing the demand spelled doom for him, ended the meeting with a lame excuse: Everyone had to leave because carpenters had to fix things in the meeting hall. Representatives of the aristocrats, religious leaders, and peasants met not inside Versailles but at a nearby tennis court, where they crafted the Tennis Court Oath, an agreement to create a constitution. (We're not making this up, people.)

The peasants believed the king would order a military crackdown as a result of this, so on July 14, 1789, mobs stormed Paris's Bastille prison to capture guns and gunpowder. This event, which began the revolution of the peasants against the monarchy and aristocracy, is celebrated today as the national French holiday Bastille Day.

About a hundred people died in the Bastille attack, including the jailer, whose head was put on a stick and paraded around Paris as a brutal symbol of the people's power. News of the revolution spread across France, and violence swept the countryside as peasants began killing nobles. Three weeks later, a newly formed government called the National Constituent Assembly banned feudalism, the age-old economic system in which peasants worked and fought for nobles in exchange for the right to farm their land. Suddenly, peasants had rights and nobles lost power.

On August 26, 1789, the new government, with help from America's minister to France, Thomas Jefferson, passed the Declaration of the Rights of Man and of the Citizen. This document declared that all French people would have the

Versailles • • Paris

FRANCE

Present-day boundaries are shown.

Corsica

ACING THE TENNIS COURT OATH

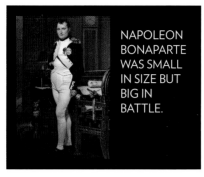

NAPOLEON BONAPARTE WAS SMALL IN SIZE BUT BIG IN BATTLE.

same rights and that "Men are born free and remain free and equal in rights," laying out in a document the fundamental principles that would guide the revolutionaries.

For the next two years, King Louis XVI and his wife, Queen Marie Antoinette, who was hated by the peasants, were virtually imprisoned in their Parisian palace, the Tuileries. Desperate to get to a small but loyal army near the Austrian border to fight the revolutionaries and take back control of their country, the king and queen plotted their escape. On June 21, 1791, just after midnight, the royal family snuck out of Paris. They were dressed as servants and had dressed their servants as royals. They didn't get too far before they were recognized—the king's face was on money, after all. King Louis and Marie Antoinette were imprisoned, and eventually the newly formed First Republic government charged them with high treason for, among other things, refusing to acknowledge the end of feudalism. On January 21, 1793, King Louis XVI was executed by guillotine. Marie Antoinette was executed later that year.

" Let them eat **cake**. "

A quote famously attributed to Marie Antoinette, but she likely never said it.

The king's death ushered in what became known as the Reign of Terror, led by French revolutionary Maximilien Robespierre. Anyone who dared disagree with Robespierre was quickly condemned to death. Within a year, close to 40,000 people were killed (including, eventually, Robespierre himself).

In the next few years, France sought to extend its power by declaring war on some of its neighbors and defeating armies in what are now Holland, northern Italy, and parts of Austria. In 1799, Napoleon Bonaparte appointed himself "first consul" and took over France's government. Five years later he crowned himself emperor of France. He would go on to conquer much of Europe and Russia. One battle he didn't win? A swarm of rabbits chased him from a celebration in 1807. Turns out, Napoleon wasn't scared of battles but bunnies.

In 1815, at the Battle of Waterloo, Britain and Prussia defeated Napoleon and finally restored peace to Europe. Close to 50,000 men died in the fighting.

So what did the French eat during revolutionary times?

THE BATTLE OF WATERLOO ENDED NAPOLEON'S RULE.

A DAY in the Life: Paris, 1793

Mon dieu, il fait très froid! (My goodness, it's very cold!) A child living in Paris, which was then Europe's second largest city, may have woken up cold and hungry in a little bed, confused as to what day and time it was. The French Republic had just forced everyone to switch to the new French Revolutionary Calendar, which had 10 days in a week, 10 hours in a day, 100 minutes in an hour, and 100 seconds in a minute. Confused yet?

Kids changed out of their night frocks and put on clothes in France's national colors of red, white, and blue. Boys wore long woolen or cotton pants and jackets, and girls squeezed into tight dresses nipped in at the waist, which made it hard to move or even take a deep breath. They then went into the small living room that might double as a kitchen to eat some cold pottage (thick veggie-and-grain stew) with stale rye or barley bread.

Most didn't go to school. Boys of rich families had tutors, while girls were taught to dance or play music. Everyone else worked as soon as they were old enough to help, whether it was taking care of horses or assisting a seamstress. Those whose *pères*, or fathers, belonged to the butcher, baker, or cheesemaker guilds would help out in those stores. Children as young as six might be sent out to earn money or food for the family. Some kids had to stand in long lines to get their family's daily bread. Families got rations of free 1.5-pound loaves with a bread card.

After an exhausting workday for some of up to 12 hours, kids would dodge the city's horses, carriages, and people and head home. They walked up as many as six flights of stairs to their apartments for their second—and last—meal of the day, supper. Lucky ones might have cheese, bread, honey, potatoes, sausage, or leftover pottage. They might then do more tasks to earn money, like sewing or making lace, toys, or dolls to sell to shops. Finally, dirty, greasy, tired, and still hungry, they'd climb into their chilly beds, wondering what would happen on the often violent streets of Paris the next day.

A BOWL OF POTTAGE

Spicing Things Up!

Up until the French Revolution, the rich and royal ate the most elaborate and exotic foods perhaps ever created, from palaces made of sugar and spices to exotic roast emu. But the rest of the country ate basic foods, much of it produce and grains. The French were big fruit eaters—strawberries, apricots, raspberries, pears—they loved it all (they usually cooked the fruits before eating them). Who planted many of the original fruit trees? The Romans, back when they called France "Gaul."

Potatoes had been introduced to France in the late 16th century but were thought only good enough for pigs to eat. Because they were cheap, though, the poor ate them. Meat was a luxury: One pound (450 g) a week per person was the legal allotment in 1793, or the equivalent of four quarter-pound burgers. The poor ate any cut of meat they could get their hands on.

Those who lived in the countryside had small plots of land to grow fruits or veggies, or shared common gardens. They could hunt or fish as long as the land wasn't owned by a noble or the church.

City dwellers had access to plenty of markets, bakeries, butchers, and cheese stores, but food was very expensive. In Paris, the central market was Les Halles, where blood flowed in the streets from animals being slaughtered by butchers.

About 70 percent of Paris's homes had three rooms or fewer. There was a salon, or living room, a bedroom, and sometimes a kitchen. Those without kitchens made meals in the living room or sometimes the bedroom.

Table matters!

In wealthy homes, dining was a formal and hours-long affair that took up much of the day. Food was served all at once family style, instead of being served in courses. Elaborate kitchens had multiple fireplaces, ovens, and copper pans. Porcelain plates, silver forks, and fancy glassware became must-haves for the rich. These extravagant dinners were adult-only affairs. Kids ate upstairs with their governesses, or nannies.

For poor families, not only was there not a dining room, but there wouldn't have been a table. Families ate sitting on a bed, a chair, or the floor, scooping food from bowls with any crusty old bread leftover from the day's allotment.

Common foods eaten in **France** at the time:

- Snails
- Animal liver, brains, or legs
- Potatoes
- Leeks
- Lentils
- Seasonal fruits and veggies
- Barley and rye bread
- Cheeses
- Pottage, soups, and stews

91

Kids in wealthy families didn't eat with their parents.

FRENCH REVOLUTION

Kitchen Tools

BECAUSE SO MANY PEOPLE ATE WARMED UP GRUEL AND STALE BREAD MOST DAYS, THERE WASN'T A NEED (OR MONEY) FOR MUCH COOKING EQUIPMENT OR TOOLS. HERE ARE A FEW OF THE MOST COMMON ITEMS A MIDDLE-CLASS HOUSEHOLD WOULD HAVE:

Charcoal-Burning Stoves

These smoky little stoves cooked food quickly, so they were good for making fish, veggies, sauces, and chicken.

Butter Crocks

Little ceramic lidded bowls that kept butter fresh.

Cutting Stump

Big sections of logs were used to butcher and chop on.

Copper Saucepots

Sauces were extremely important to the French (who invented béarnaise, béchamel, and others), and they used specific small copper pots to make them.

Strainers

To make their beloved sauces, the French ladled liquids into large wire mesh strainers to make them velvety smooth.

Despite the glittering appearance of Versailles, guests complained that the stench from the poorly built latrines made the enormous palace smell of poop!

Up until the revolution, uneaten table scraps of meat were collected from the rich and sold to the poor. No wonder left-overs got a bad reputation!

MENUS OF THE
Rich & Famished

While people living outside the palace ate mostly scraps and old hunks of bread, Marie Antoinette always ate like the queen she was. Here is part of a menu that was served at Versailles on July 24, 1788:

Rice Soup, Croutons with Lettuce, Rump of Beef with Cabbage, Loin of Veal on the Spit, Spanish Pâtés, Grilled Mutton Cutlets, Rabbits on the Skewer, Fowl Wings, Turkey Giblets in Consommé, Larded Breast of Mutton with Chicory, Fried Turkey, Sweetbreads, Calves' Heads, Chickens à la Tartare, Spitted Suckling Pig, Fowl with Consommé, Rouen Duckling with Orange, Fowl Fillets en Casserole with Rice, Cold Chicken, Chicken with Cucumber, Fillets of Rabbit, Breast of Veal on the Spit, Shin of Veal in Consommé, Cold Turkey, Chickens, Capon Fried with Eggs and Breadcrumbs, Leveret, Young Turkey, Partridges, Rabbit

THE BIRTH OF THE RESTAURANT

When we eat at a restaurant we feel restored, right? Funny, because that's the meaning of the French word "restaurant." It's been used since medieval times to describe a meaty broth that restores you to health. In 1765, a shopkeeper in Paris served not just a restaurant but also a leg of lamb, which gave rise to the new idea of going to a place called a restaurant. People could sit at their own table, read a list of available foods written on a piece of paper or a blackboard, and choose what to eat. While inns, cafés, and taverns had long existed, their diners had to sit at shared tables with strangers and eat whatever was served; there were no choices. The restaurant was a radical departure and very quickly became a favorite place for anyone who could afford it.

By the Numbers

14.5 SOUS*:
Cost of a 4-pound (1.8-kg) loaf of bread.

18 SOUS*: Average weekly wage of a laborer.
*7 sous equaled about 2 cents at the time.

100: Number of restaurants in Paris before the revolution.

500 TO 600: Number of restaurants in Paris after the revolution.

60: Average amount of eggs a person ate annually in France in 1790.

170: Average number of eggs a person eats annually in France today.

At the time of the revolution, France was the world's largest producer of sugar (which was grown in their Caribbean colonies), yet the French ate a little less than 2 pounds (900 kg) of sugar per person annually. In England, the average was more than 15 pounds (6.8 kg) per person per year in 1792.

Eat THIS

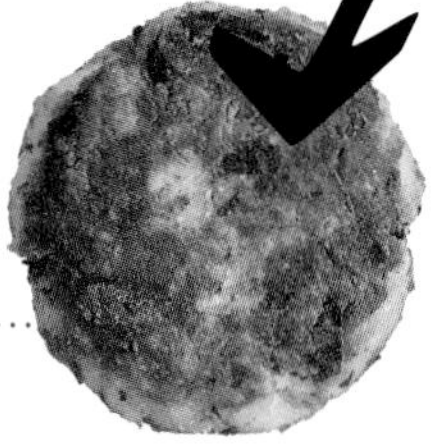

REVOLUTIONARY POTATOES

This recipe is lightly adapted from one in *La Cuisinière Républicaine,* published in 1795 by Madame Mérigot. She called it "Pommes de Terre a l'Econome," or "Thrifty Potatoes," but it sure tastes rich.

Makes 12 Servings

2 pounds (900 g) large baking or Idaho potatoes, peeled and sliced

3 sprigs parsley, finely chopped, or 2 teaspoons dried parsley

3 scallions, finely chopped

2 shallots, peeled and finely chopped

2 cups (280 g) finely chopped cooked meat (sliced ham, turkey, or chicken breast are good options)

2 tablespoons melted butter (30 ml)

Salt and pepper to taste

1 egg

1/2 cup (57 g) whole wheat flour

3 tablespoons (45 ml) olive oil

Chopped parsley to garnish

1 Ask an adult to bring a large pot of water to a boil over high heat. Cook the potatoes until tender when pierced with a fork, about 10 minutes. Ask an adult to drain the water out. Mash with a fork or potato masher and let cool.

2 Meanwhile, in a large bowl, combine the parsley, scallions, shallots, and meat together.

3 Add the mashed potatoes to the meat mixture, along with the butter, and mix well. Salt and pepper to taste. Shape into 12 medium-size patties.

4 Beat the egg in a bowl with a little water. Place the flour on a plate or bowl. Dip the patties in the egg and let the excess egg drip off, then lightly roll them in flour, again shaking off any excess flour.

5 Ask an adult to warm 1-1/2 tablespoons oil in a large non-stick sauté pan over medium-high heat. Ask an adult to cook half the patties, turning after 5 minutes. Cook 4 minutes more, or until dark brown on both sides. Repeat with remaining olive oil and patties. (You can also cook these in a 350°F/177°C oven for 20 minutes.) Garnish with parsley and serve.

" It's potatoes and meat—what's not to like? "
Lahav, 14

LET THEM EAT QUICHE

This eggy pie can have almost anything added to it, from ham and mushrooms to broccoli and kale. You can use any cheese you like and try different types of spices. It's also great the next day.

Makes 6 Servings

1 9-inch deep-dish frozen piecrust

1 tablespoon (15 ml) olive oil

1 shallot, peeled and chopped finely

4 large eggs

1 cup (240 ml) heavy cream or half-and-half

Pinch ground nutmeg, salt, pepper, and cayenne pepper

1 cup (125 g) grated cheddar, Swiss, or any cheese you like

1 10-ounce (284-g) package frozen chopped spinach, defrosted and squeezed to drain water

1 Ask an adult to preheat the oven to 400°F/204°C. Prick the bottom of the piecrust with a fork and ask an adult to bake it for 10 minutes. Ask an adult to remove from the oven and reduce the heat to 350°F/177°C.

2 Meanwhile, ask an adult to warm the olive oil in a small sauté pan over medium-low heat. Add shallots and cook until soft, about 3 minutes. Set aside to cool.

3 While the crust is pre-baking, in a large bowl, whisk the eggs, cream, nutmeg, salt, pepper, and cayenne pepper.

4 Place the pie shell on a large baking sheet. Add the shallots to the crust, then the cheese and spinach. Gently pour the eggs on top and ask an adult to place in the oven and bake for 50 minutes, or until it's set (when you stick a knife or fork into the middle, it will come out clean) and the top is lightly golden.

> "You can make quiche savory and healthy all at the same time, which is amazing. This works well with a mix of cheeses. I also liked it with ground sausage and minced garlic. It was delicious.
> Myka, 14

POP CORNY quiz

1
What was collected from the rich and sold to the poor?

A. Lupines
B. Table scraps
C. Pens
D. Laptop computers
E. Very large refrigerators

2
Who was thought (inaccurately) to have said, "Let them eat cake"?

A. Marie Antoinette
B. Big Bird
C. Thomas Jefferson
D. You
E. Albert Einstein

3
How much did a loaf of bread cost?

A. Almost as much as King Louis XVI spent in an hour
B. Almost as much as the ear of a parrot
C. Almost as much as a laborer earned in a week
D. Almost as much as the Xbox back then
E. Almost as much as a large dinosaur bone

4
Where did most Parisians cook and eat their meals?

A. In their enormous fancy kitchens
B. In their tiny kitchens/ living rooms
C. In their elaborate backyard gardens
D. On the rooftops of their stately homes
E. On staircases

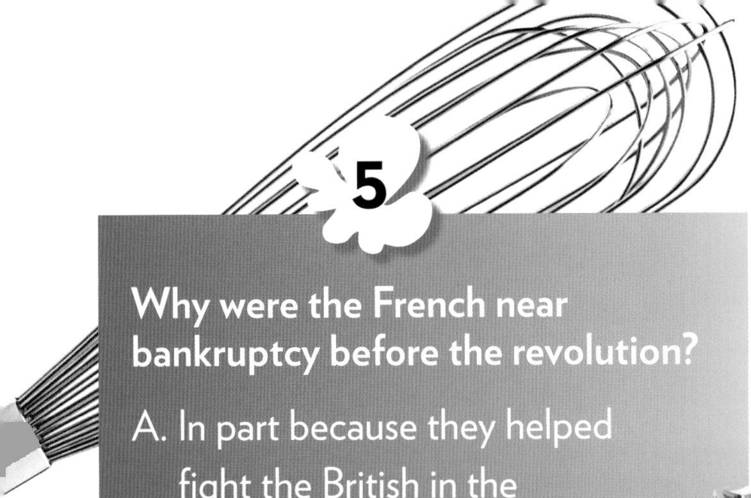

5

Why were the French near bankruptcy before the revolution?

A. In part because they helped fight the British in the American Revolution

B. In part because nobles didn't pay taxes

C. In part because only the poor paid taxes

D. In part because of excessive spending by the crown

E. All of the above

Ugh! You're squishing me!

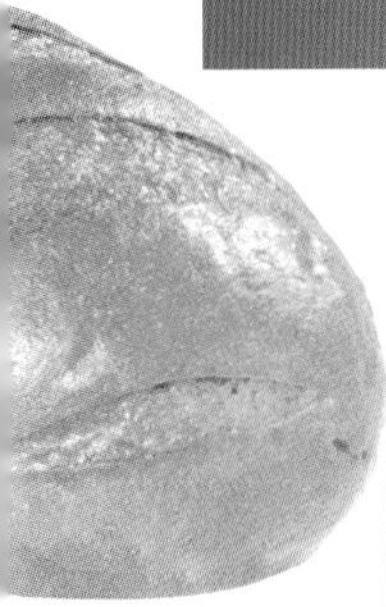

7

Where did France's representatives agree to create a constitution?

A. On a tennis court

B. In a hot-air balloon, which had just been invented

C. On a beach

D. In a swimming pool

E. At the dog park

6

Who helped influence the creation of the Declaration of the Rights of Man and of the Citizen?

A. Thomas Jefferson

B. Ivan the Terrible

C. Maximilien Robespierre

D. Louis XVI

E. Taylor Swift

Answers: 1. B; 2. A; 3. C; 4. B; 5. E; 6. A; 7. A

97

The Industrial
Revolution:
Children and Machines Enter the Workforce En Masse

A BITE-SIZE history

While people in America and France were dumping tea and rioting for bread, there was another revolution going on, but this one was technological and happening largely in Great Britain. Some historians say achievements from this period, known as the industrial revolution, between about 1760 and 1840, were the most important in history after prehistoric man's discovery of fire and the domestication of animals and plants.

From steam power to gas lighting, stoves to canned foods, the world changed faster during the industrial revolution than it had in more than a thousand years. But despite these inventions, not everyone's life improved. Things were especially hard for children, who became a major part of the workforce. And starvation remained common even though food was more widely available.

One of the first major changes to come from the industrial revolution was in clothing and fabric manufacturing. Until the early 1740s, cotton was made by hand on a spinning wheel that produced thread and yarn. A series of mechanical improvements to the wheel—one involved a donkey and another was called a spinning jenny—enabled people, and eventually mills filled with people, to make clothes and other textiles cheaper and faster. This brought the cost of clothing down, making it more widely available to more people.

Probably the most important invention during the industrial revolution was the steam engine. Before steam, people, wind, water, and animals powered machines. But then Scotland's James Watt created a steam pressure gauge in

A SPINNING JENNY

Present-day boundaries are shown.

SCOTLAND

UNITED KINGDOM

NORTHERN IRELAND

IRELAND

ENGLAND

WALES

•London

the 1780s, as well as a rotary engine that allowed machinery to run on its own. Watt figured out how many horses his engine replaced, creating the measurement "horsepower" to explain engine strength. One advantage of his discoveries? Factories could now be built anywhere because they weren't dependent on water or wind.

The replacement of candles and oil lamps with gas lighting, which started in London around 1812, was also an important development. People could now work at night in factories (boo, hiss), walk the streets safely at night (yay!), and hit the newly bustling cafés and theaters (double yay!). Gas lighting in homes followed slowly, likely because it was pricey to install.

In 1804, Richard Trevithick built the first steam-powered locomotive for the Penydarren Ironworks. It traveled between the Welsh towns of Merthyr Tydfil and Abercynon. In 1863, an underground railway was built in London, which became the world's first subway.

With trains and ships now using steam engines, things could be delivered relatively quickly anywhere in the world. That included people. Travel was faster and easier than ever; this was convenient for Great Britain's Queen Victoria, who, having ascended the throne in 1837, ruled 25 percent of the world's population, including Australia, Canada, India,

LIGHTING UP THE NIGHT WITH GAS LANTERNS

Hong Kong, and Kenya. She reigned for 63 years.

Other major achievements during the industrial revolution included the first flushing toilet (1775), a machine that produced large plate glass (early 1800s), and a new type of cement (1824), which is still used today. An early version of photography also developed during this era, forever changing how people saw the world.

With so many inventions, new factory jobs were created. And huge numbers of people moved to cities to work in the factories or open businesses. Families began to earn more money, and the middle class grew. So some people's lives got easier. But most who worked in factories (which the English poet William Blake called "dark satanic mills") labored for low wages and often in dangerous and unhealthy conditions. You know who many of those workers were? Kids.

Instead of getting a good education, many children, some as young as five, were expected to work, and for only a tenth of an adult's wages. Many kids died in accidents at the factories or from diseases caused by malnutrition. The writer Charles Dickens helped shine a light on this horrible way of life in his books *Oliver Twist* and *David Copperfield*. After public outcry, Britain's

> "Our **regular time** was from five in the morning till nine or ten at night; and on Saturday, till eleven, and often twelve o'clock at night, and then we were sent to **clean the machinery** on the Sunday. **No time was allowed for breakfast** and **no sitting for dinner** and **no time for tea.**"
>
> **John Birley, former child worker at Cressbrook Mill, England**

Parliament passed laws in 1833 and again in 1844 prohibiting children younger than nine from working. Tough luck for anyone 10 and up!

The Industrial Revolution was a complicated era; but there were definitely some amazing improvements with food!

KIDS HEADING TO THE FACTORY

A DAY in the Life: London, 1822

"It can't be 4 a.m. already!" That's what children might have thought waking up before the sun in a cramped two-room apartment in a crowded, dirty building with no running water. They would have splashed some cold water on their faces, dressed in dirty, torn shirts and pants or long cotton dresses and headed to the cold, filthy, loud factory. Kids had to be there at 5 a.m. and worked until at least 8 p.m., six days a week.

They were given three small meals a day at the factory, which they often ate standing up while they worked. Typical foods included oatcakes, gruel, porridge, mutton, bread, and soup. Some factories like the St. Pancras Workhouse in London had long dining tables but no plates, knives, or forks. Oatcakes and other items were served into the fronts of boys' shirts while girls used their dirty aprons to hold their meager bites. They were given few, if any, rest breaks.

Children's jobs might be anything—making matchsticks, cleaning chimneys, working in a coal mine, labeling packages, apprenticing at the baker's, or picking fruit. But no matter what they did, one thing was for sure—children made only a tiny bit of money (about four pennies a day), worked at least 12 hours a day, were sometimes beaten or punished, and were exhausted, hungry, and dirty by the end of every day.

They would trudge home to their crowded apartments through dark and dangerous streets (gas lamps were only just starting to pop up on Britain's streets in the 1820s). Children might kiss their parents good night and fall into bed, only to repeat the same hard routine the next day.

WORKERS AT A WOOL MILL

Spicing Things Up!

Thanks to improved transportation and new technologies, people could have just about any food or ingredient they wanted—if they had the money. From North American salt cod to South American salt beef, the world was the wealthy's oyster ... and their mussels and their salmon.

One ingredient that wasn't readily available? Potatoes. In Europe, the potato crop had contracted a disease in the mid-1840s. It was a particular disaster for Ireland's poor, who relied on potatoes as a staple in their diet. About one million Irish died from starvation or sickness, and another two million left the country seeking relief from what became known as the Great Famine. Additionally, more than 300,000 Prussians, Belgians, and Dutch died as a result of the potato blight.

Even though access to ingredients had improved, people weren't necessarily eating better than ever before. Many struggled just to buy milk and bread at stores, and they weren't able to get their own food by gardening, fishing, or hunting, as they lived in cities.

Running water was still rare (water was obtained outside, often out of a spigot in the yard), so kitchen sinks weren't common. And kitchens were often still used not just for cooking but also as living areas and bedrooms. Poorer families sometimes divided the kitchen into two rooms by hanging a curtain down the middle.

In wealthy homes, the kitchen table doubled as a servant's workstation and dining table. In middle-class kitchens, families spent a lot of time at the table, the same as today.

Table matters!

In poor homes, there were no table manners as there were often no tables. People ate most of their meals at work, no matter their age. In wealthy homes, it was all about manners. Children didn't eat with their parents but with their governess or nanny.

Kids who were at the table were expected to be seen and not heard and to speak only when spoken to—not like the fun and frolic that happens at tables today!

Common foods eaten in **Great Britain** at the time:

- Oatcakes
- Gruel
- Porridge
- Potatoes and other root vegetables like carrots and turnips
- Bread
- Bottled beans, vegetables, and fruits
- Cheese
- Sheep trotters
- Rice milk
- Bacon
- Treacle
- Mutton

A girl works with a flock of turkeys.

INDUSTRIAL REVOLUTION
Kitchen Tools

THERE WAS A DRAMATIC IMPROVEMENT IN KITCHEN TOOLS AND EQUIPMENT BETWEEN THE LATE 1700S AND LATE 1800S. HERE ARE JUST A FEW:

Pasteurization

In 1864, Louis Pasteur created a sterilization process (they named it after him!) that killed harmful bacteria in dairy products like milk and gave the foods a longer shelf life. Pasteurization is still used today in many dairy products and some prepared foods.

Stoves

Between 1800 and 1860, the open hearth cooking that had been used for thousands of years was finally replaced. The cast-iron standing stove became must-have equipment for just about everyone to cook on. The super-handy invention also proved useful for laundry (clothes were boiled on top of the stove) and heating the home.

Canning

In the late 1700s, Nicolas Appert came up with a way to preserve food for the French military. He placed food in a jar, sealed it with cork and wax, and boiled it. In 1810, he made the technique public. It was the first time food could be easily preserved and stored in large quantities.

Eggbeaters

These hand-cranked mixers enabled cooks to quickly whisk and beat eggs, which made baking easier.

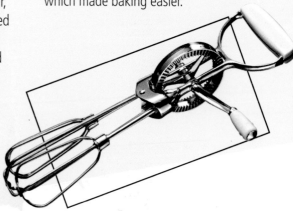

MENUS OF THE
Rich & Famished

This menu, written in ever-so-fashionable French, included 4 soups, 5 fish dishes, 4 appetizers, 11 entrées, 8 sides, and 13 desserts. It was served to Queen Victoria at Buckingham Palace on a summer evening. Wonder what the occasion was—maybe the birthday of one of her favorite dogs?

Soups: À la Cressy, À la Tortue, À la Royale, Riz au Consommé, Fish Le St. Pierre à la sauce Homard, Les Gougeons frits sauce Hollandaise, Les Filets de Soles à la Ravigotte, Le Saumon sauce aux Capre, La Darne d'Esturgeon au beurre de Montpellier

Small Plates: Le Piece de Boeuf à la Flamande, La Pate-chaud de Pigeons à l'Anglaise, Les Poulardes et Langues aux Choux-fleurs, La Noix de Veau en Bedeau

Entrées: Les Cotelettes de Mouton à la purée d'Artichauts, Les Boudins de Laperaux à la Richelieu, Les Pieds d'Agneau en Canelons farcis à l'Italienne, Les Filets de Poulardes à la Régence, Les Tendons de Veau glaces à la Macédoine, Les Petits timbales de Nouilles à la Purée de Gelinottes, Les Combattants, Les Chapons, L'Oie, Roast Beef, Roast Mutton, Hashed Venison

Spiced Food: Les Beignets au Parmesan, Les Petits Pois à la Francaise, Les Haricots Verts à la Maître d'hôtel, La Gelée au Vin de Champagne, L'Aspic de Volaille à la Belle-vue, Les Fonds d'Artichauts à la Provençale, Les Concombres farcis à l'Essence, Plum and Yorkshire Puddings

Dessert: La Cascade Ornée de Sucre File, La Chaumiere rustique, Le Buisson d'Ecrivisses, La Crème au Caramel, Les Petits Gateaux de Crème Anglaise, La Tourte de Peches, Les Choux-fleurs à la sauce, Le Bavarouix de Fraises, La Gelée de Peches, Les Tartelettes de Cerises, Le Gateau de Pethiviers, Le Pudding de Riz, Le Baba au Rhum

YUCKY
HABITS
OF YORE

When kids ate in the factories they worked in, grease, dust, wool, chemicals, and dirt often got on and in their food. They had little choice but to eat it anyway.

By the Numbers

25: Average number of courses Queen Victoria's court ate each day! Five courses were served for breakfast, eight or 10 for lunch, and the same number for dinner!

50 POUNDS (23 kg): Average amount of coal families needed for their stoves every day.

38–60%: Average amount of income spent on food in 1824 in Britain.

One of Queen Victoria's favorite foods was raized pie: A turkey stuffed with a chicken stuffed with a pheasant stuffed with a woodcock, all wrapped in pastry and baked as a pie.

In 1762, England's Earl of Sandwich claimed to have invented or inspired the first sandwich. As the story goes, the earl asked his butler to bring him something he could eat without a fork so he didn't have to stop playing cards. Of course, there have been sandwich-like foods throughout history, but the idea of eating meat between two pieces of toast is attributed to him.

Eat THIS

OLIVER TWIST'S OAT CAKIES

"Please, sir, I want some more." That famous line from *Oliver Twist* will be what you say after trying one of these warm from the oven. If you want them to be more like oatmeal raisin cookies, we recommend adding 1/2 cup of raisins and cooking the cookies two minutes longer. Live in an egg-free, gluten-free household? Make these swaps: For the egg, use 1/2 teaspoon flaxseed with 2 tablespoons applesauce; for the all-purpose flour, use all-purpose gluten-free flour; and for the whole wheat flour, substitute 3 tablespoons each of oat flour and coconut flour.

Makes About 12 Cakes

1 stick (113 g) unsalted butter, at room temperature

1/2 cup (100 g) dark brown or light brown sugar (packed)

1/4 cup (50 g) granulated sugar

1 large egg

1/2 teaspoon (2.5 g) salt

1/2 teaspoon (1.1 g) cinnamon or nutmeg

1/4 teaspoon (500 mg) baking soda

1/2 tablespoon (7.5 ml) vanilla extract

1/4 cup plus 2 tablespoons (47 g) all-purpose flour

1/4 cup plus 2 tablespoons (47 g) whole wheat pastry flour

1-1/4 cups (175 g) old-fashioned rolled oats

1 Ask an adult to preheat the oven to 350°F/177°C. Use a large nonstick cookie sheet or line a large cookie sheet with parchment paper and set aside.

2 In a large bowl, cream the butter and sugars with an electric mixer on high speed until smooth, about 3 minutes. Add the egg and beat until incorporated, scraping the bowl as necessary. Add the salt, cinnamon, baking soda, and vanilla and mix at medium speed until blended. Add the flours, slowly adding each as you go, until both are integrated. Stir in the oats and mix. (If you're using raisins, add them now.)

3 Using a heaping 2 tablespoons of dough per cookie, form into balls and press down gently to form circles. Ask an adult to transfer to the oven and bake about 15 minutes or until cookies are nearly set and light golden brown. Ask an adult to remove from the oven and let cool for a minute or two before diving in!

> " I think they have a nice chewy/crunchy contrast, as well as a sweet-and-salty mix that appeals to most people. "
> Maddie, 14

THE EARL OF SANDWICH SANDWICH

We made ours a little tastier than what the earl probably ate, but we used some ingredients that he probably had— cheddar cheese and roast beef. You can substitute with your favorite cheese and meat, poultry, or fish if you prefer.

Makes 1 Serving

2 slices whole wheat or whole grain bread

1 tablespoon (14.4 g) butter or olive oil, at room temperature

2 slices (38 g) cheddar or any other cheese you like such as Swiss, jack, or mozzarella

2 slices (56 g) roast beef, ham, turkey, tuna, or smoked salmon

Salt and pepper

1 Ask an adult to warm a nonstick sauté pan over medium heat. Butter (or use olive oil) one side of both slices of bread.

2 Place one slice of bread, buttered side down, in the pan. Top with the cheese and the roast beef. Season to taste. Place the other slice of bread on top, buttered side facing up.

3 Cook for 2 minutes or until light golden, lightly pressing down with the spatula, then turn over and cook 2 minutes more, lightly pressing down with the spatula, until lightly brown. Cut in half and say, "Thanks, Earl of Sandwich!"

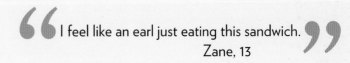

" I feel like an earl just eating this sandwich. "
Zane, 13

POP CORNY quiz

1

What jobs did kids often do during the industrial revolution?

A. Work in the coal mines
B. Work in the factories
C. Work as a farm hand
D. Work as an apprentice
E. All of the above

3

How much might a kid earn in a day?

A. 10% of an adult's earnings
B. 18% of an adult's earnings
C. 532% of an adult's earnings
D. 2,000% of an adult's earnings
E. 7,357,000% of an adult's earnings

2

How many pounds of coal might it take to feed a family's stove every day?

A. 3.5 pounds (1.5 kg)
B. 43 pounds (19.5 kg)
C. 50 pounds (23 kg)
D. 387 pounds (175 kg)
E. 266,287 pounds (120,786 kg)

4

What was a major invention that changed the way people ate?

A. The railroad
B. Canning
C. Stoves
D. Pasteurization
E. All of the above

Um, you can count me out of this dinner party!

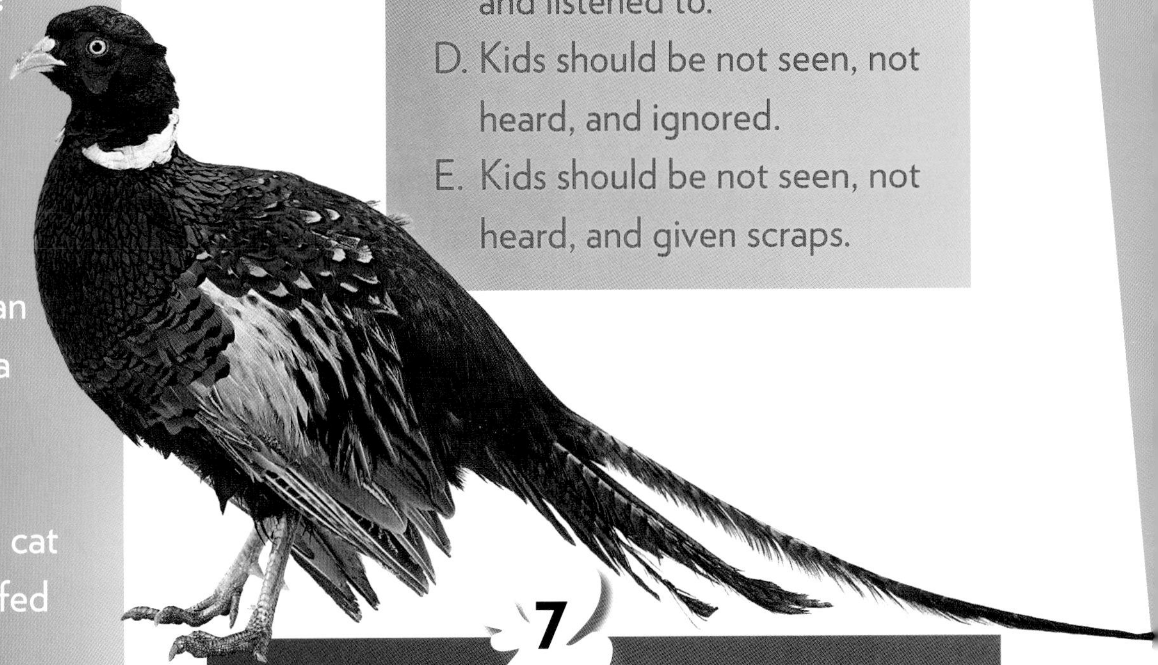

5

What was a raized pie?

A. A woodcock stuffed in a pheasant stuffed in a chicken stuffed in a turkey

B. A mouse stuffed in an armadillo stuffed in a cheetah stuffed in an elephant

C. A spider stuffed in a cat stuffed in a dog stuffed in a horse

D. A pheasant stuffed in a wild boar stuffed in a lion stuffed in a rhino

E. A rabbit stuffed in a leopard stuffed in a lion stuffed in a giraffe

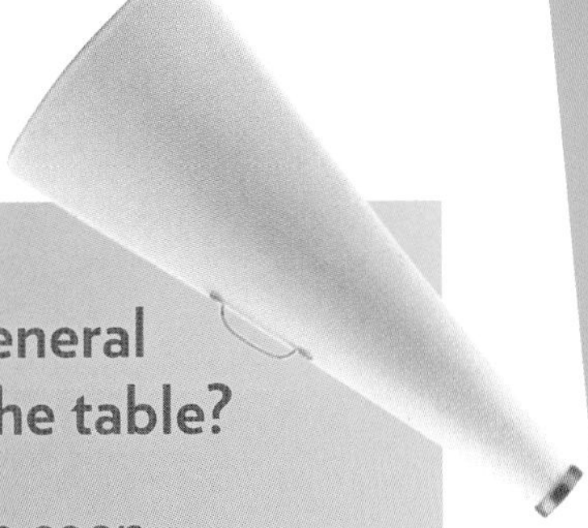

6

What was the general rule for kids at the table?

A. Kids should be seen and heard.

B. Kids should be seen and not heard.

C. Kids should be seen, heard, and listened to.

D. Kids should be not seen, not heard, and ignored.

E. Kids should be not seen, not heard, and given scraps.

7

How did some people make their kitchen into two rooms?

A. Painted a line down the middle of the floor

B. Put two stoves in the room

C. Hung a curtain in the middle

D. Decorated each side differently

E. Called each side something different

World War I:
Hatred and Hunger Spread

A BITE-SIZE
history

There was nothing great about the Great War, as it was eventually called. World War I was one of the deadliest wars in history. It lasted from July 28, 1914, to November 11, 1918, and in that time about 11 million soldiers and seven million civilians died. Twenty million more people were wounded.

Present-day boundaries are shown.

ROMANIA
HUNGARY
AUSTRIA
GERMANY
BELGIUM
UNITED KINGDOM
FRANCE
PORTUGAL
LUXEMBOURG
ITALY
SERBIA
GREECE
RUSSIA
BULGARIA
JAPAN
OTTOMAN EMPIRE (not a present-day country)

It was the first time that so many countries—32 in all—went to war against each other. One side was known as the Allied powers and included France, Great Britain, Russia, Serbia, Belgium, Japan, Portugal, Romania, Greece, Italy, and the United States. The other side was called the Central Powers and included Germany, Austria-Hungary, the Ottoman Empire, and Bulgaria.

It all started with another shot heard around the world—this one was the assassination of Archduke Franz Ferdinand, heir to the Austro-Hungarian Empire. After visiting a hospital in Sarajevo on June 28, 1914, he and his wife, Sophie, were killed by a Serbian nationalist who wanted to end Austria's political and economic dominance over Serbia. One month later, the Austro-Hungarian Empire declared war on Serbia. This triggered a chain reaction throughout Europe: Russia backed Serbia; Germany invaded Belgium, which brought Great Britain into the war as they had a treaty with Belgium; and then Germany invaded Luxembourg and France. Eventually, battle lines were drawn throughout Europe.

Much of the fighting was concentrated in northern France in an area called the western front. Battles raged there, with armies hidden in long lines of trenches. They fought each other with tanks, grenades, bombs, and poisonous gas.

THE ASSASSINATION OF FRANZ FERDINAND

Men from all of the warring countries joined the military. Even children helped in the war effort. In Britain, a 12-year-old named Sidney Lewis famously lied about his age so he could fight. (Some say there were 250,000 British soldiers under 19, the legal age for service.)

Meanwhile, U.S. president Woodrow Wilson had promised the American people that the country would stay neutral, a position that most agreed with even after a German submarine sank the British passenger ship *Lusitania* in 1915, killing 1,198 civilians, including 128 Americans. Alfred Vanderbilt, one of the world's richest men, was among the casualties.

The war raged on for three years, throwing dozens of countries into tumultuous and terrible times. This was especially true for Russia when, in 1917, a series of revolutions by radical Bolsheviks led to Tsar Nicholas II stepping down from his throne. He and his family were subsequently killed by a Bolshevik firing squad. The Bolsheviks became known as Communists after that event.

On April 6, 1917, the United States finally declared war on Germany. More than two million American soldiers would head to the front in France.

In the meantime, because of widespread food shortages across Europe and the fact that U.S. troops had to be fed,

POSTERS AT THE TIME ENCOURAGED PATRIOTISM.

the government created the U.S. Food Administration to manage America's food supply chain. Led by Herbert Hoover, the organization did not ration food but encouraged voluntary conservation. Americans leapt to the challenge and reduced their food consumption by 15 percent between 1918 and 1919. The result? 18,500,000 tons of food were sent to millions of war-ravaged European soldiers and citizens.

With America helping the Allies, the Germans eventually agreed to an end to the war. On November 11, 1918, an armistice was agreed to. (We still celebrate Armistice Day, but now we call it Veterans Day.) The Treaty of Versailles that formally ended the war was signed at none other than King Louis XVI's gold-encrusted Versailles Palace on June 28, 1919, exactly five years to the day that the archduke had been assassinated.

World War I was devastating: Millions died, were starving, or displaced from their homes; country borders were redrawn; empires ended, including the Ottoman, German, Russian, and Austro-Hungarian; and new countries were created, including Czechoslovakia and Yugoslavia.

During this time of intense conflict and sadness, what did people eat? Not that much, it turns out.

> **Hunger** does not breed **reform**; it breeds **madness**.
>
> **President Wilson in an address to Congress on Armistice Day, Nov. 11, 1918**

Because they were fighting the Germans, Americans renamed some German foods; for instance, **frankfurters** became known as liberty dogs.

HELPING HOOVER IN OUR U.S. SCHOOL GARDEN
KIDS DID THEIR PART.

A WOUNDED SOLDIER GETS HIS DUE.

A DAY in the Life: Chicago, 1917

"Boy am I hungry!" That's what kids might have thought as they woke, remembering all of the tasty breakfast foods they had eaten just months ago, before the United States had entered the war and didn't need to save most of its food for others.

Children might have gotten dressed alone in their little brick homes because their dad might be at war and their mom might already be at work—many women worked in factories, farms, and charities for the war effort.

They might have grabbed a bowl of a new cereal called Kellogg's Bran Flakes and gone to school—finally, every state in the country had a law requiring children to go to school. After class, while dodging the Model T cars that were becoming popular and munching on new cookies called Oreos, kids might have gone to volunteer at a community garden, pick up unwanted clothes to send overseas to war refugees, or help at the local Red Cross. And on their way home, they might have passed a hotel that had that fancy new thing called a telephone.

At dinner, families might have sat in the kitchen eating canned beef stew with turnips harvested from the garden. Perhaps another Oreo would be dessert. Kids might have taken their comic books to bed and said a prayer for those in Europe dealing with the Great War at their doorsteps.

BOYS IN A 1917 SHOP CLASS

Spicing Things Up!

During this time, eating—or not eating—was a patriotic act. Food could be a weapon in the war, so the more people saved and sacrificed, the more food went to soldiers and war victims. Food was one way everyone could do their part to win the war. Posters that read "Food will win the war" were everywhere.

Americans were asked to eat less meat, sugar, fat, and wheat and more perishable items such as fruits and veggies. To conserve, Meatless Monday and Wheatless Wednesday campaigns were started. Local women's clubs and the media helped Americans learn how to can and preserve their produce. People called all of this food saving "Hooverizing" after Herbert Hoover, who would go on to become president in 1929.

There was also a push to grow food on both private and public lands. Americans were asked to "sow the seeds of victory" and be "soldiers of the soil." Some of the crops were sent overseas and some fed people at home. By the end of the war, more than five million victory gardens grew in the United States.

As the war dragged on, meat, dairy, and even produce became increasingly harder to get, especially in Europe. In Britain, a system of ration books with stamps for purchasing certain scarce food items meant that no matter how rich someone was, they couldn't get more than their fair share—even King George and Queen Mary used them. Anyone caught stealing ration books or making fake ones was imprisoned.

The kitchen became less a place for long hours of tedious work and keeping the stove going; it was now a room to get a quick meal. Almost all middle-class homes had a stove, sinks with running water, and an icebox (literally a lined wooden box that held ice and was used for food storage), or maybe a refrigerator. One-fifth of American homes even had electricity. Kitchens were beginning to look like ones we would recognize today.

The way people purchased food was also changing. For centuries, people visited individual markets—the greengrocer (the produce store), bakery, fishmonger, cheese store, or butcher. Shopping lists were handed to clerks, who brought items to the counter. But all that changed in 1916 when Clarence Saunders opened a store in Memphis, Tennessee, called Piggly Wiggly. There, shoppers could pick up the food themselves—there were 600 items to choose from—and bring it to a counter to pay. Grocery shopping eventually became cheaper because of these changes since fewer employees were needed to fill shoppers' orders.

Table matters!

In some circles, good dining etiquette continued, with hands washed, children quiet and calm, and formal place settings on the table each night. But in most homes during World War I, family dining habits started to fall apart because more moms worked, families had different schedules, and food was scarce.

Common foods eaten in the United States at the time:

- Canned tuna and other fish
- Canned meat
- Liberty dogs with liberty cabbage
- Peanuts
- Bananas
- Potatoes
- Cornmeal
- Oatmeal
- Cornflakes and cold cereals
- Canned soups
- Canned fish
- Fresh and canned fruits and veggies

PEA SOUP

CHOICE QUALITY

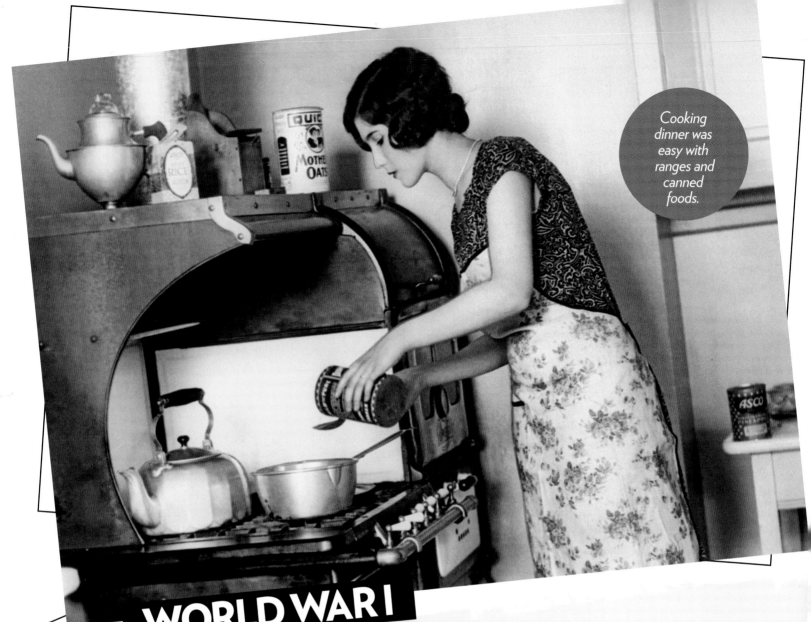

Cooking dinner was easy with ranges and canned foods.

WORLD WAR I

Kitchen Tools

COOKING BECAME EASIER FOR THE HOME COOK THANKS TO SOME COOL NEW TOOLS THAT INCLUDED:

Waffle Irons
This easy-to-use appliance created crusty square pancakes called waffles.

Cooking Ranges
Now common in homes, these had a gas or electric cooktop and an oven below in one handy unit.

Toasters
Bread could be warmed up in this machine, which had been invented in 1909.

Refrigerators
An electric version of the icebox, refrigerators were introduced to consumers in 1914.

Drippings (fat) from cooking beef or other meats were used in the manufacture of explosives.

As food became more scarce in Britain, it was rumored some butchers sold cat meat.

A wartime dish from Hawaii's newspaper *Maui News* featured sliced bananas dressed in mayonnaise and finely crushed walnuts.

By the NuMBers
DAILY FOOD RATION FOR A BRITISH SOLIDER:
- 20 ounces (567 g) of bread (about 1 loaf)
- 3 ounces (85 g) of cheese
- 1/2 cup jam
- 1 cup vegetables

254,000:
Miles of train tracks that crisscrossed the U.S. in 1916. Food could now travel speedily across the country.

MENUS OF THE
Rich & Famished

There weren't many fancy gatherings going on during the war, but on the rare occasion someone threw a party, they might serve a popular icebox or refrigerator cake. "An absolutely new confection is the refrigerator cake, which is being served occasionally at parties in Kansas City when the hostess takes a vacation from Hooverizing, for the ingredients are expensive," wrote someone in the *Kansas City Star* on October 19, 1917. "The unique feature is that no baking is required, and the cake is served cut in wedge-shaped pieces like pie." The recipe demonstrates that refrigerators weren't very cold at the time, as the cake needed to be chilled for 30 hours!

In 1918, the first book focusing on calories was published: *Diet and Health: With Key to the Calories* by Dr. Lulu Hunt Peters.

Horses were fed before soldiers on the front lines in World War I.

SOME PRODUCTS AMERICANS EAT TODAY WERE INVENTED IN THE 1910S:
- **Breakfast:** Aunt Jemima Pancake Flour, Quaker Puffed Rice, Kellogg's All-Bran
- **Snacks and Convenience Foods:** Domino Sugar, Hellman's Mayonnaise, Mazola Corn Oil, Oreos, Life Savers, Moon Pies, Contadina Tomato Sauce

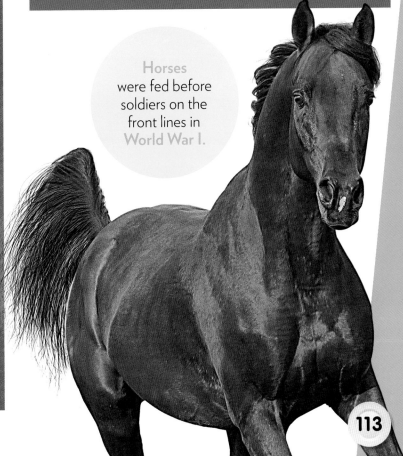

Eat THIS

THE ARMY'S NON-GHOULISH GOULASH

The Doughboy Cookbook from the Quartermaster Corps features this Army Goulash, which we adapted. Originally made with canned beef (nicknamed "canned horse," "bully beef," or "monkey meat"), this would be tasty in a roll, on top of mashed sweet potatoes, or served with wild rice, quinoa, or whole wheat pasta.

Makes 6 Servings

1 tablespoon (15 ml) olive oil

1 medium onion, peeled and chopped

1 pound (454 g) ground beef

1 15-ounce (427 g) can beans (black, pinto, or cannellini), drained and rinsed

1-1/2 cups (340 ml) tomato sauce

1 teaspoon (2.6 g) chili powder

Salt and pepper

1 Ask an adult to warm the olive oil in a large sauté pan over medium heat. Add the onion and cook until softened, about 4 minutes.

2 Add the beef and cook, stirring until browned, about 8 minutes. Add in the remaining ingredients and simmer on low heat, stirring occasionally, for 30 minutes. Season to taste. Eat it in the mess (slang for an army's dining room), but don't make a mess!

" The whole family liked this recipe. "
Olivia, 14

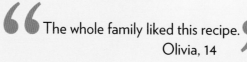

114

ALLIED SOLDIER PUDDING

This no-egg recipe, inspired by the Milk Biscuit Pudding from *Feeding Tommy* by Andrew Robertshaw, fed 100 soldiers at a time. It's scaled down here and adapted for modern times. We recommend using plain or tea biscuits, which were similar to what was used back then, but any hard cookies or biscuits can be substituted.

Makes 4 Servings

Butter, for greasing pan

2 cups (200 g) crumbled tea, digestive, plain, or whole wheat biscuits

1-1/4 cups (312 ml) milk

1 tablespoon (15 ml) honey

1/2 cup (75 g) raisins

1 teaspoon (2.6 g) cinnamon

2 tablespoons (12 g) grated lemon or orange zest, plus a squeeze of lemon or tablespoon of orange juice

Vanilla Greek yogurt or ice cream, for topping

1 Ask an adult to preheat the oven to 350°F/177°C. In a food processor, crush the biscuit crumbles into crumbs. Transfer to a large bowl.

2 Add the remaining ingredients into the bowl and stir until completely incorporated. Transfer to a large greased cake pan (9 x 9 inch/23 x 23 cm) and cook for 35 minutes or until set. Serve warm with yogurt or ice cream.

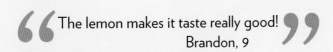

❝The lemon makes it taste really good! ❞
Brandon, 9

POP CORNY quiz

1

What was the fat from cooked beef and other meats used for?

A. To make greasy homes
B. To make explosives
C. To make Slip 'N Slides
D. To make wax paper
E. To make fat cow figurines

2

How much did Americans reduce their food consumption by between 1918 and 1919?

A. 0.00000003373735451%
B. 0.7363649393%
C. 0.3837375%
D. 15%
E. 23,384,625%

3

What was the name of the first self-service grocery store?

A. Smiggly Giggly
B. Liggly Figgly
C. Piggly Wiggly
D. Tiggly Biggly
E. Ciggly Higgly

4

What day was invented to promote food conservation?

A. Meatless Monday
B. Toothless Tuesday
C. Witless Wednesday
D. Throwaway Thursday
E. Frighten Your Cat Friday

I ... I am a liberty dog.

6

What is Hooverizing?

A. Saving food to help the war effort
B. Vacuuming
C. Slang for chasing criminals when J. Edgar Hoover ran the FBI
D. Devouring your dinner
E. The experience of riding a hovercraft

7

Which snack or cookie was invented during this time?

A. Ding Dong
B. Pop Rocks
C. Kit Kat
D. Oreo
E. Fig Newtons

5

What were liberty dogs?

A. A new name for pooches with freedom
B. A new name for sausages/hot dogs
C. A new name for dogs that took liberties
D. A new name for very large puppies
E. A new name for Snoopy's friends

America's
Great Depression:
Breadlines, the Dust Bowl, and a Crashing Economy

A BITE-SIZE history

The period after World War I from 1920 to 1929 is now known as the Roaring Twenties. This decade saw a skyrocketing economy and stock market; falling prices on important items like cars, radios, and washing machines; women cutting their hair short and calling themselves flappers; and a craze for a type of music called jazz. It was a vibrant time when artists and writers were celebrated and a new kind of film called a "talkie" debuted—instead of reading captions and listening to piano music, the audience could actually hear actors speak on screen. What a concept!

But the "anything goes" attitude of the Roaring Twenties came crashing down on October 29, 1929, a day that would be forever known as Black Tuesday.

The national economy had been weakening for several reasons, including agricultural problems, higher debt, less regulation of the banking industry, and lower taxes. A panic on Wall Street that day sent the stock market into a nosedive. About $25 billion—equal to about $320 billion today—was lost. Overnight, millions of companies became worthless and investments vanished. Many people went bankrupt in just hours.

This economic collapse started a vicious cycle: companies closed, people lost their jobs, and spending decreased, which caused more companies to close. The financial health of the United States had a ripple effect across the world: Once America's economy began to unravel, a worldwide depression spread like a virus.

NORTH DAKOTA
SOUTH DAKOTA
NEBRASKA

UNITED STATES

KANSAS

OKLAHOMA

TEXAS

Present-day boundaries are shown.

A NEW YORK CITY BREADLINE

From 1929 to 1933, more than 100,000 businesses failed and one-quarter of the population was out of work in the United States. Half of all families were living at or below the poverty line. More than 11,000 banks—almost 50 percent—went bankrupt and closed, taking people's money with them.

Herbert Hoover, who had managed the nation's food supply during World War I, was now president. But he felt the federal government shouldn't create jobs or provide direct economic assistance to citizens. People became desperate, homeless, and hungry. Charities set up daily soup kitchens; lines were hundreds deep and hours long just for a free loaf of bread. There were riots, with the hungry and poor smashing grocery store windows to steal food. Shantytowns known as "Hoovervilles" sprang up in the middle of many cities as homeless people tried to survive day to day. Much of this misery was documented by talented authors like John Steinbeck, F. Scott Fitzgerald, and Margaret Mitchell and photographers like Margaret Bourke-White, Dorothea Lange, and Walker Evans.

At the same time the stock market crashed, a severe drought ravaged farmland in the middle of the country. The fertile soil had declined in quality from overuse,

ACTOR CHARLIE CHAPLIN PLAYS A WWI SOLDIER.

creating what became known as the Dust Bowl. The region, which stretched from Texas through Oklahoma, Kansas, Nebraska, and the Dakotas, also suffered from a lack of trees and water. Enormous black clouds of topsoil rolled across the country, sometimes making it all the way to the East Coast. Thousands of farmers abandoned their land and headed West. California began receiving about 7,000 migrants a month.

In the 1932 presidential election, New York governor Franklin Delano Roosevelt defeated President Hoover. Roosevelt won, in part, because of his optimistic, can-do attitude, declaring in his 1933 Inaugural Address "that the only thing we have to fear is fear itself."

Roosevelt created a program called the New Deal, which focused on three R's: relief for the poor and unemployed; recovery for the economy; and reform to the banking industry and the stock market. Roosevelt regularly updated Americans with radio addresses called fireside chats. Broadcast from near a fireplace in the White House, his chats helped people feel more confident that they would get through the difficult times.

New government programs, from insuring people's bank accounts to creating Social Security, which provides monthly income to the elderly, sick, and poor, began. A minimum wage and maximum work hours were established; a Food Stamp Plan, which gave vouchers for purchasing food to the poor, started up; and the Works Progress Administration put eight million people back to work building dams, highways, bridges, and parks for a monthly salary of $41.

By injecting billions into the economy, creating jobs, and setting up reforms and safety nets, Roosevelt, who was elected to four consecutive terms as president (he died in his fourth term), helped lead the country out of the Great Depression. So how did people find enough to eat? It was tough.

A DAY in the Life: Oklahoma, 1932

"Why do I have so much dust in my mouth?" That's what kids might have thought when they woke up in their little ranch homes in Oklahoma in the early 1930s, as dust storms ravaged the parched earth. Life was tough: There was more dust than food, few families had work, and the land was hard to farm.

Kids would put on their clothes, many of which were made from flour or feed sacks, and then scrounge around for scraps of last night's dinner before heading to school with a lantern (in case a dust storm caused a virtual blackout) and lunch pail in hand. As they sat in a one-room schoolhouse organized in rows by age, they did math and reading exercises. When a dust storm hit, they all stayed inside the increasingly dark schoolhouse, putting wet towels over their mouths.

After school, kids might head to a friend's house to listen to the popular radio comedy show *Amos 'n' Andy*. Or they might walk into town for food (with that lantern) and stand in a long line for some bread and soup. The line might snake past a movie theater showing the Marx Brothers, Charlie Chaplin, or Shirley Temple films. Not many had the 35 cents for a ticket, though.

At night, children would climb into their dusty beds, perhaps dreaming of a place called Hollywood, where the focus was on making talkies and not dust storms.

A DUST STORM HITS KANSAS.

MANY FAMILIES LIVED IN TENTS.

Spicing Things Up!

While there wasn't rampant starvation during the Great Depression, half the country struggled to put food on the table every day, so the poor ate whatever the soup kitchen or breadline handed out or what was sold at the Penny Restaurant, a dining hall where a meal could be had for a penny or two.

Those who owned land were encouraged to grow charity or work-relief gardens, and many donated produce to soup kitchens; there were even baskets at New York's Grand Central Terminal and Pennsylvania Station for people to donate homegrown fruit and vegetables.

For those who could afford it, large-scale self-service stores, which now had new inventions called shopping carts, were becoming the norm. There were fewer bakers, butchers, and fishmongers because Americans were beginning to prefer faster and processed food to fresh ingredients.

The middle class ate pretty much as it had before but switched to less expensive cuts of meat such as feet, liver, and other organs. Potluck parties and luncheons instead of fancy dinners were common. Convenience foods—soda, chips, candies, canned fruits—became a bigger part of the diet. These ultramodern foods were thought to be more sanitary, fresher, and vitamin-enriched, despite the fact that many of them were very unhealthy.

Casseroles and one-pot dishes like pot pies became all the rage because you could throw just about every ingredient—canned or frozen—into one dish and bake it, which meant less clean up and kitchen time.

The kitchen was changing, too. It was beginning to be thought of as another room in which to display style and personality. Many were decorated with Fiestaware, a ceramic dinnerware that came in reds, greens, and yellows. "Iceless" refrigerators were commonplace, and stoves were now available in colors like mint and yellow. People might display china on shelves or have linoleum floors that matched other furnishings and rooms.

Table matters!

During the Great Depression, when families ate at home, they often ate in the kitchen at a little table. Because parents struggled to make money, they took any job and any shift possible, so eating meals together wasn't always possible.

Table etiquette was still important, though, in most homes. Children were expected to be quiet and behave and wait for their parents to begin eating before they did. Anyone who misbehaved might be sent to their room without dinner.

Common foods eaten in the United States at the time:

- Canned vegetables and fruits
- Frozen fish
- Canned fish and meat
- Candy
- Chips
- SPAM
- Canned and powdered soup mixes
- Small game, like rabbits, squirrels, and gophers
- Sandwiches with just mayonnaise, ketchup, or sugar
- Bread

To improve his reputation, infamous Chicago gangster Al Capone opened soup kitchens like this one, which fed more than 3,000 hungry Chicagoans each day.

GREAT DEPRESSION

Kitchen Tools

DESPITE THE POVERTY OF MANY, THIS ERA SAW A LOT OF LIFE-CHANGING ITEMS BECOME WIDESPREAD, INCLUDING:

Sliced Bread

Invented in 1928, the first nationally available presliced bread was sold by Wonder. For the first time kids could quickly grab a slice rather than cut a piece with a bread knife.

Frozen Food

After Clarence Birdseye learned how Canada's Inuit used ice to freeze just-caught fish, he invented a way to flash freeze veggies and fish to retain their texture, vitamins, and flavor.

Iceless Refrigerators

At the start of the Great Depression, electric refrigerators were in just 8 percent of homes, but by the end of the 1930s, they were in almost half. No longer did families need a weekly ice delivery. Now they could store frozen foods next to the ice tray, ensuring they had something easy peasy to prepare whenever they wanted it.

TODAY
CRACKED WHEAT   1¢
BARLEY CEREAL   1¢
BEAN SOUP   1¢
POSTUM COFFEE   1¢
RAISIN COFFEE   1¢
SOAKED PRUNES   1¢
SEEDLESS RAISINS   1¢
WHOLE WHEAT BREAD   1¢
CREAMERY BUTTER   1¢
COLD MILK   3¢
LENTIL SOUP   1¢

YUCKY HABITS OF YORE

People who lived in the Dust Bowl often kept their bread in a drawer to keep the dust off of it.

MENUS OF THE
Rich & Famished

Because none but the wealthiest had maids or cooks, most grand dinner parties ceased during the early 1930s. Women cooked dinners—or at least heated up frozen ones. People were more likely to go to a restaurant for a celebration; those with less money switched to hosting luncheons or teas, serving menus such as this 1932 *Ladies' Home Journal* version:

Saturday Luncheon Menu

Chilled Tomato Cocktails, Salmon Loaf, Molded Potato Salad, Hawaiian Coleslaw, Olives, Spiced Sekel Pears, Watercress-and-Lettuce Sandwiches, Buttered Nut Bread, French Peach Pie, Hot Coffee, Grape-Juice Lemonade, Milk

One place extravagance was still on view? Luxury cruises, where no expense was spared for the wealthy. Here is a dinner menu from one that sailed in 1930:

The N.Y.K. Line S.S. *Fushimi Maru* Dinner Menu

1st Course: Hors d'Oeuvres
2nd Course: Consommé Xavier, Potage Avoine
3rd Course: Fillet Mullet, Lobster Sauce
4th Course: Lamb Escalopes with Spinach, Boiled Corned Brisket of Beef with Red Cabbage
5th Course: Roast Loin of Pork, Apple Sauce, Roast Chicken & Bacon, Potatoes, Boiled Carrots
6th Course: Pudding à la Leopold, Wine Jelly, Butter Cream Cakes
7th Course: Devilled Biscuits
8th Course: Assorted Nuts, Raisins, French Plums, Pears, Apples, Demitasse
9th Course: Cold Buffet of Roast Veal and Bologna Sausage

By the Numbers
PENNY RESTAURANTS in
New York City fed **10,000** people a day in 1933. Here's what you got:

- **FOR 1 CENT:** Soup, cracked wheat, steamed cornmeal, steamed oatmeal, steamed hominy grits, bread pudding, stewed prunes, stewed raisins, honey, milk, tea, raisin bread, black coffee, whole wheat doughnut, and two slices of whole wheat bread or whole wheat raisin bread
- **FOR 3 CENTS:** Meat cake, fruit salad, 1/2 grapefruit, sliced peaches, a whole wheat crumb cake, lettuce and tomatoes, and tuna fish salad

20 CENTS AN HOUR:
Salary that high school student Alvin Apetz made as a part-time janitor, and it "was pretty good money in them days," he said.

The first free school lunch program began in 1936. By 1942, more than five million kids were receiving free lunches.

Hundreds of foods that are still around today were invented during the 1930s. Here are just a few:

- **Candy & Chocolate:** Tootsie Pops, Snickers, Twizzlers, 3 Musketeers, Heath Bar, Kit Kat, Chunky chocolate bar, Mars Almond Bar, Fifth Avenue, Nestlé chocolate chips
- **Baked Goods & Breads:** Krispy Kreme doughnuts, Hostess Twinkies, Wonder Bread, Bisquick, Pepperidge Farm bread
- **Snacks & Chips:** Frito-Lay corn chips, Lay's potato chips, Ritz Crackers, Skippy Peanut Butter, Mott's Apple Sauce
- **Dinners:** Campbell's Chicken Noodle and Cream of Mushroom soups, Kraft Macaroni & Cheese, Oscar Mayer wieners, SPAM, Birds Eye meat and fish entrées, Beech-Nut baby foods
- **Condiments:** Kraft Miracle Whip, Heinz Ketchup
- **Beverages:** Royal Crown Cola, 7 Up, Orangina, Hawaiian Punch
- **Brands:** Goya, Betty Crocker, Carvel, SPAM

Eat THIS

RAG SOUP

A classic recipe during the Great Depression, this was usually made with spinach, broth, and macaroni or noodles. We added a few more veggies to make it even healthier. You could also add chicken, shrimp, fish, chopped sausage, beef, or pork to make it heartier. Just don't put any old clothes into it, please!

Makes 6 Servings

1 tablespoon (15 ml) olive oil

1 small onion, peeled and chopped

1 small carrot, peeled and sliced

1 garlic clove, peeled and minced

3 cans (14.5-ounce/1.3-L) low-sodium chicken broth

1 cup (237 ml) water

1-1/2 cups (115 g) egg noodles

1/2 teaspoon (350 mg) dried basil or rosemary

1/2 teaspoon (1 g) turmeric

Salt and pepper to taste

1 Ask an adult to warm the olive oil in a large stockpot over medium heat. Add the onion and cook for 2 minutes. Add the carrot and garlic and cook for about 4 minutes.

2 Add in the chicken broth and 1 cup water. Bring to a boil. Add the egg noodles and spices, salt, and pepper and simmer on low heat for about 15 minutes. Serve with the Up-in-the-Clouds Bread (page 150) or Hippocrates' Favorite Barley Bread (page 35).

> **"** The soup was light and simple with mild spices that work very well together. We tossed in some fresh spinach leaves and it was yummy. **"**
> Brynna, 16

PAUPER POT PIE

Makes 6 Servings

1/2 stick (57 g) butter

1/4 cup (30 g) all-purpose flour

1 cup (237 ml) low-sodium chicken broth

1 small onion, peeled and chopped

1 clove garlic, peeled and minced

3 medium carrots, peeled and thinly sliced

1/2 cup (75 g) frozen petite peas

2 cups (250 g) cooked, chopped chicken

Salt and pepper

1 homemade or store-bought refrigerated or frozen piecrust (top and bottom)

1 egg yolk

While pot pies had long been popular, they had a resurgence in the United States during the Great Depression because almost any combination of canned or frozen foods could be thrown in. One junior recipe tester recommends serving this with steamed asparagus. Whether you use ramekins for individual pies or a regular piecrust, you will want to rename this Rich Pot Pie as it tastes like a million bucks!

1 Ask an adult to preheat the oven to 400°F/200°C, and then ask an adult to melt the butter in a large sauté pan over medium heat. Whisk in the flour and cook, and continue whisking, for 1 minute. Add the broth and cook, stirring, for 2 minutes or until thickened. Add the onion and garlic and cook for 2 minutes or until slightly softened. Add the carrots and peas and cook for another 3 minutes. Add in the chicken and cook, stirring, for 3 minutes. Season with salt and pepper.

2 Ask an adult to transfer the hot chicken filling into a prepared piecrust bottom or pastry, lining a buttered 9-inch (23-cm) pie pan, with the excess dough trimmed off. (You can also use 6 individual ramekins.)

3 Cut out a 9-inch round with the remaining piecrust dough and place on top of the pie. Using a fork, seal the pastry edges together.

4 In a small bowl, combine the egg yolk with 2 tablespoons of water. Brush over the piecrust with a pastry brush or spoon.

5 Put the pie pan or ramekins on a large baking sheet and ask an adult to place it in the oven and bake for about 30 minutes or until the pastry is golden brown. Ask an adult to remove it from the oven and let cool for 2 minutes before eating.

" We will never eat frozen pot pie again. I love the flavor and did not know this is so easy to make. "
Jasmy, 11

POP CORNY quiz

1

Where did people in the Dust Bowl sometimes keep their bread?

A. In their computer bag
B. Behind their ears
C. In their drawers
D. Between their toes
E. In their microwave

2

How much money was lost in the stock market crash on Black Tuesday in 1929?

A. $3
B. $17.83
C. $1,203,472
D. $25 billion
E. $125 billion

3

Which food product was introduced during the 1930s?

A. Skippy Peanut Butter
B. Ritz Crackers
C. Kit Kats
D. SPAM
E. All of the above

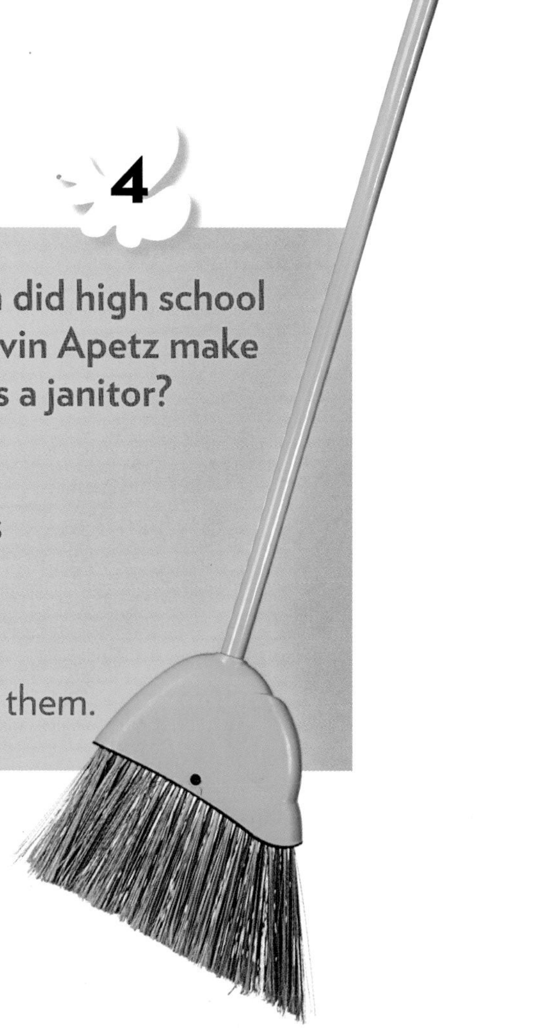

4

How much did high school student Alvin Apetz make per hour as a janitor?

A. 2 cents
B. 20 cents
C. $7.43
D. $25
E. He paid them.

5

Who is considered the father of frozen foods?

A. Clarence Birdsong
B. Clarence Birdseye
C. Clarence Birdsbeak
D. Clarence Birdsfeet
E. Clarence Birdsbone

6

What did Roosevelt say in his Inaugural Address?

A. The only thing we have to fear is fear itself.
B. The only thing we have to fear is a smelly sock.
C. The only thing we have to fear is a large lizard.
D. The only thing we have to fear is a mouse with a bad cold.
E. The only thing we have to fear is a giraffe that wants to read with us.

7

How many times was Roosevelt elected president?

A. 1
B. 2
C. 4
D. 19
E. 64

Now that's a stretch!

The World at
War, Again:

Food Rations, Victory Gardens, and Patriotic Pies

A BITE-SIZE history

POLAND
CZECHIA (CZECH REPUBLIC)
GERMANY
UNITED KINGDOM
FRANCE
SPAIN
ITALY
AUSTRIA
SLOVAKIA
ETHIOPIA
SOUTH AFRICA
RUSSIA
CHINA
JAPAN
AUSTRALIA
NEW ZEALAND

Present-day boundaries and names are shown.

A fter one world war and a global depression, few imagined that another world war would occur—but that's exactly what happened. World War II remains the deadliest in human history; millions of people perished at the hands of the Nazis, and more than 60 million are believed to have been killed overall, the majority of them civilians. The war involved hundreds of millions of people from about 100 countries and ended only when atomic bombs were dropped on Japan. Food was rationed, women entered the workforce like never before, and patriotism and sacrifice were the order of the day.

World War II officially started in 1939, but many earlier conflicts led up to it, including Japan invading China in 1931, Italy invading Ethiopia in 1935, and a civil war in Spain in 1936 in which Germany and the Soviet Union (as Russia was then known) provided weapons and forces to opposing sides.

In 1933, a former World War I soldier named Adolf Hitler became chancellor of Germany. He got rid of the democratic government, ordered weapons to be made and stockpiled, and began expressing racist views to the public. In 1938, his army took over Austria and the German-speaking parts of Czechoslovakia. In March 1939, Germany invaded the rest of Czechoslovakia and prepared to invade Poland.

The Germans and the Soviets, led by Joseph Stalin, formed an alliance in August 1939 agreeing not to fight each other and to divide Poland and other parts of Eastern Europe. This alliance cleared the way for Germany's invasion of Poland on September 1.

EVEN THE YOUNGEST AMERICANS LEARNED ABOUT RATIONING DURING WORLD WAR II.

Two days later, France and the United Kingdom declared war on Germany; other countries with ties to the British Empire (including Australia, Canada, New Zealand, and South Africa) soon followed suit. They were known collectively as the Allied powers. Germany quickly took control of much of Europe and formed another alliance with Italy and Japan. They called themselves the Axis powers.

By May 1940, Germany had invaded France, which soon surrendered; then Germany set its sights on Britain. After trying several strategies, Germany began brutal bombing attacks on London and other British cities, in what became known as the Blitz. British prime minister Winston Churchill and King George VI proved to be calm, steady leaders during the Blitz, which was crucial to the British people. Both men helped keep morale and determination up while the country singlehandedly battled Germany.

On another war front, in June 1941, Germany broke its nearly two-year-old alliance with Stalin and invaded the Soviet Union in one of the war's most brutal battles, with millions dying on both sides.

President Roosevelt had been promising to keep the United States out of the war, but at the end of 1940 he declared that the U.S. was the "Arsenal of Democracy" and began supplying weapons to Britain.

And then came "a date which will live in infamy."

On December 7, 1941, the Japanese bombed the U.S. naval base at Pearl Harbor, Hawaii, killing 2,403 American soldiers and wounding 1,178. The next day, the United States declared war on Japan. Three days after that, on December 11, it declared war on Germany and Italy.

With the United States at war with Japan, some worried that Japanese Americans might be loyal to their ancestral homeland instead of America. So President Roosevelt unfairly ordered more than 120,000 Japanese Americans to internment camps across the United States. Even though they were U.S. citizens, they were held as prisoners until the war ended.

Finally, a turning point occurred for the Allies on June 6, 1944. Led by the United States, the Allies invaded German-occupied France on Normandy's beaches in what is now known as D-Day (which is a military term that refers to a day of attack). By the end of the day, more than 150,000 Allied troops had landed in Normandy and begun to push the Germans out of France. Another 350,000 Allied troops landed in France during the next two weeks.

In early 1945, the Allies, which now included the Soviet Union, invaded Germany. That April saw the deaths of many key players in the war: President Roosevelt passed away, and Vice President Harry Truman took over; Hitler killed himself; and Italy's leader Benito Mussolini was murdered. On April 29, 1945, German forces began to surrender. But Japan did not.

So on August 6, 1945, the United States dropped the world's first atomic bomb on Hiroshima, Japan. The second was dropped on Nagasaki, Japan, three days later. The bombs killed 220,000 people and left many more sick from radiation poisoning. That same day, the Soviet Union entered the war and quickly overran Japanese forces in Manchuria. Devastated, Japan surrendered on August 15, 1945. The war was finally over.

After six years of war, hundreds of millions of lives had been destroyed, cities lay in ruins, and people were starving. The world would never be the same. During this very dark time, how and what did people eat?

> " This is a food war. "
>
> Lord Woolton, Britain's minister of food, 1941

food
1- buy it with thought
2- cook it with care
3- use less wheat & meat
4- buy local foods
5- serve just enough
6- use what is left
don't waste it
U.S. FOOD ADMINISTRATION

A DAY in the Life: San Francisco, 1942

"Sigh." Kids in the United States in 1942 woke up in a country now at war, and it affected every single person. This was especially true on the West Coast in cities such as San Francisco, where whole neighborhoods were suddenly empty because of the internment of Japanese Americans.

Children might have left their beds and found themselves alone in their houses. Many mothers now worked for the war effort, while many fathers were away in the military. Kids would squeeze into hand-me-down clothes (few had new clothes because fabrics were being used for everything from parachutes to military uniforms). Maybe they had some dry Cheerios (milk was in short supply) before heading to school. Lessons might be interrupted by air-raid drills in which everyone got under their desks or lined up against the wall in the hallway in case there was an enemy bombing. (Of course, this would not have saved anyone, but it made people feel like they were doing something to protect themselves.)

After a free school lunch and more classes, kids might tend the victory gardens in the schoolyard. Even though television had been invented in the late 1920s, few people actually owned them, so for entertainment kids went to the movies to see Mickey Mouse or Bambi. Or maybe they went to someone's home to listen to Edward R. Murrow's radio reports about the war live from London.

Moms might still be at work at dinnertime, so some children made their own dinners—maybe some fresh veggies from the school garden or canned fish on sliced bread and a piece of victory cake. Then it was back to bed to dream of happier times ahead.

A WAR RATION BOOK

THE ATTACK ON U.S.S. *CALIFORNIA* AT PEARL HARBOR

BOYS AND GIRLS IN THEIR VICTORY GARDEN

Spicing Things Up!

Making do with less. Ration books. Victory gardens. Does that all sound familiar? World War I, the Great Depression—much of the first half of the 20th century was about sacrificing to help others. As in World War I, food was needed for the soldiers during World War II, and Americans again went without, learning to bake cakes without eggs and eating meals without meat or wheat. Coffee, sugar, eggs, butter, meat, milk, fish, and cheese were all rationed. Steak, chicken, and turkey were scarce because it all went to the soldiers. Cheaper cuts of meat were available, but you had to know how to cook them to make them taste good.

Rationing in America began again in April 1942 and didn't end until June 1947. Sugar and rubber tires (which were needed for military vehicles) were rationed first; other foods and gas followed. People learned to make do: Instead of sugar, local honey or molasses was used; instead of wheat, there was barley or oats. Affordable white bread filled out many meals. Even the White House abided by the rations; a diary notes that First Lady Eleanor Roosevelt once served salt fish four days in a row. And President Roosevelt found himself eating a lot of liver and green beans, which he loathed, and drinking less coffee.

During World War II, most kitchens looked pretty much as they had in the 1930s, if maybe a bit more decorated. Beige linoleum floors, green cabinetry, and wooden furniture were all the rage.

Because little food was transported—trucks, trains, and gas went to the war effort—people either ate what was locally grown or new, highly processed convenience foods, be they canned, frozen, or boxed. With women working in such large numbers, time to shop, prepare meals, and clean up was scarce. Those convenience foods were a big help.

Once again, victory gardens were a part of the war effort. Almost 20 million gardens were planted everywhere, from vacant lots to rooftops, schoolyards to windowsills. Even Mrs. Roosevelt grew one on the White House grounds.

Table matters!

For many households, family mealtimes and etiquette were not observed: People ate at different times because of their new schedules.

KIDS WORKING ON THEIR ROOFTOP VICTORY GARDEN

Common foods eaten in the **United States** at the time:

- White bread
- Packaged cereals
- Local seasonal fruits and veggies
- Canned and frozen produce
- Cheap cuts of meat
- Canned meats and fish
- Canned beans
- Frozen foods
- Candy bars

Children were seen and heard at dinnertime in the 1940s.

The **first frozen complete dinners** were invented in 1945 by Maxson Industries for service on aircrafts. The idea (and the food) was improved and introduced **four years later** to the **home cook.**

WORLD WAR II
Kitchen Tools

AMAZING TECHNOLOGIES WERE INVENTED DURING THE 1940S, INCLUDING THE FIRST MICROWAVE (WEIGHING IN AT 600 POUNDS [272 KG]), THE CROCK-POT, AND THE TRASH COMPACTOR. BUT NONE OF THESE WERE AVAILABLE TO THE HOME CONSUMER UNTIL AFTER THE WAR.

An official government order banned wartime production of 80 different appliances so that all metals, including aluminum and cast iron, and plastic went toward war efforts; home cooks relied on the tools they had from the 1930s.

YUCKY HABITS OF YORE

During the horrific **Siege of Leningrad**, Germany tried to **starve** the Soviet city into submission. More than 1.5 million **people died** in two and a half years. Desperate citizens resorted to **eating sawdust, toothpaste**, and even **licking dried paste** off of wallpaper.

MENUS OF THE Rich & Famished

Everyone had to use rations, so even the rich couldn't dine extravagantly. Here's a sample buffet menu from the 1942 *Wartime Entertaining* guidebook: Chicken Pie de Luxe, Fresh Green Salad, Assorted Rolls or Baking Powder Biscuits, Jam and Relish Tray, Chilled Fresh Fruit, Honey Drop Cookies, Coffee or Tea.

More than one-third of American women worked during the war. The Rosie the Riveter "We Can Do It" poster encouraged them.

Just like in the 1930s, a lot of food products we still have today were invented during this decade. Here are just a few:

- **Beverages:** Red Cheek Apple Juice, frozen orange juice, V8 Cocktail Vegetable Juice, Nestlé Instant Tea, Nestlé Quik
- **Snacks:** Dairy Queen soft serve ice cream, Dannon Yogurt, Cheetos, Sara Lee Cheesecake, Rice Krispies Treats
- **Candies:** M&M's, Junior Mints, Almond Joy
- **Cereals:** Cheerios, Kellogg's Raisin Bran, Post Corn Toasties
- **Convenience Foods:** Kraft Parmesan Grated Cheese, Pillsbury Pie Crust mix, frozen french fries, Ragú spaghetti sauce, French's Instant Mashed Potatoes, Reddi-wip, Minute Rice, Kraft Sliced American Cheese, Arnold Bread

By the Numbers

1.5 POUNDS (680 g): Average amount of white bread Americans ate per week. Today, we eat far less.

9 TONS (8.2 t): Amount of vegetable seeds sent for British victory gardens in 1941.

1 MILLION TONS (907,185 t): Produce grown in victory gardens in the United States during World War II.

2 POUNDS (900 g): Weekly American meat ration for adults.

American soldiers who were stateside (in the U.S.) knew they could stop by any United States Organization (USO) cafeteria and be fed well in a festive atmosphere. Here's what one canteen served on just one weekend:

- **6,300** doughnuts
- **2,340** ice-cream cups
- **2,300** cakes
- **1,475** hot roast beef sandwiches
- **1,700** pies
- **1,250 POUNDS** (567 kg) of hot dogs
- **450 POUNDS** (204 kg) of cookies
- **300 GALLONS** (1,136 L) of milk
- **185 POUNDS** (84 kg) of coffee
- **75 POUNDS** (34 kg) of popcorn, potato chips, and pretzels

Eat THIS

VICTORY GARDEN SOUP

This classic veggie soup was a great way to use up yummy vegetables from people's victory gardens. Serve this with Up-in-the-Clouds Bread (page 150) or a toasty trencher (page 55).

Makes 8 Servings

2 tablespoons (30 ml) olive oil

1 large onion, peeled and chopped

3 carrots, peeled and chopped

1 potato, peeled and chopped

1 garlic clove, peeled and minced

1 cup (150 g) fresh or frozen peas or edamame

1 cup (175 g) fresh or frozen corn kernels

2 quarts (1.8 L) low-sodium chicken broth or vegetable broth

2 tablespoons (30 ml) apple cider vinegar or fresh lemon juice

Salt and pepper

2 tablespoons (6 g) chopped cilantro or parsley

1 Ask an adult to warm the olive oil in a large stockpot over medium heat. Add the onion and cook for 2 minutes. Add the carrots and potato and cook for 4 minutes.

2 Add the garlic, peas, and corn and cook for 2 minutes. Add the broth and vinegar and cook on low heat for about 20 minutes. Season with salt and pepper and cilantro. Divide into bowls.

> "This soup was one of the best recipes I have ever tasted. It was so fun to make!"
> Ava, 11

ROSIE THE RIVETER'S CHOCOLATE BREAD CUSTARD

A 1941 advertisement for White House brand evaporated milk declared "Now create creamier custards the modern thrifty way" and featured this recipe. It tastes like a chocolate pudding cake—we adapted it slightly, but you'll still love tasting it. Consider serving it with whipped cream, ice cream, berries, or vanilla Greek yogurt.

Makes 8 Servings

1/2 cup (50 g) unsweetened cocoa powder

1/2 cup (100 g) sugar

1/4 teaspoon (1.6 g) salt

1-1/2 cups (355 ml) water

2 tablespoons (28 g) butter, plus more for greasing the pie dish

1 cup (250 ml) evaporated milk

1 cup (90 g) unseasoned bread crumbs

2 eggs, lightly beaten

1 teaspoon (5 ml) vanilla extract

Pecans for topping (optional)

1 Ask an adult to preheat the oven to 375°F/190°C. Grease a large pie dish with butter. In a large pot, mix the cocoa, sugar, salt, and water over medium heat, stirring, and with an adult's help, bring to a boil. Lower the heat, add the butter, milk, and bread crumbs, and stir. Once the butter melts, take off of the heat.

2 Let cool for a few minutes. Meanwhile, in a small bowl, combine the eggs and vanilla. Add a little of the cocoa mixture into the eggs-vanilla mixture. Add all the eggs-vanilla mixture back into the cocoa mixture and stir well. Pour into a greased 9-inch (23-cm) pie pan. (Top with pecans if using.) Put the pan into a larger pan, pour hot water in the larger pan until it goes halfway up the pie dish, and ask an adult to transfer to the oven and bake for 35 minutes or until set. Spoon up and serve!

" Razzle-dazzling raspberries raise Rosie the Riveter's Chocolate Bread Custard to a new record of deliciousness. "
Roisin, 12

POP CORNY
quiz

1

What percentage of women in America worked during the war?

A. None
B. 7%
C. 33%
D. 97%
E. All

MORE WOMEN MUST WORK

America at war needs 18 million women in full-time jobs

2

Which foods were rationed?

A. Eggs
B. Butter
C. Milk
D. Coffee
E. All of the above

3

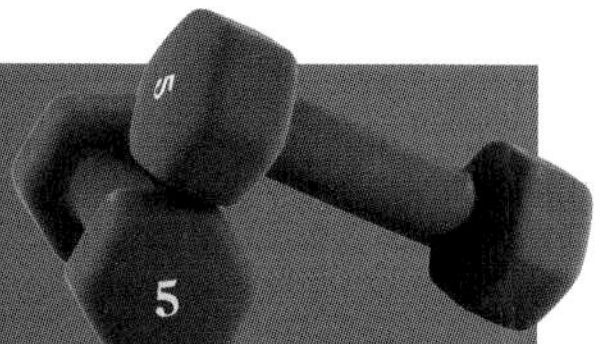

How much did the first microwave weigh?

A. 0.25 pound (113 g)
B. 7 pounds (3 kg)
C. 600 pounds (272 kg)
D. 2,503 pounds (1.135 kg)
E. 1 billion pounds (907 million t)

4

What was Rosie the Riveter's slogan?

A. We Can Do It
B. You Can't Do It
C. Why'd You Do It?
D. How'd You Do It?
E. Who Do It?

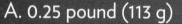

5

During World War II, which of these things happened?

A. More than 60 million people were killed.

B. Hundreds of millions of people were involved.

C. About 100 countries participated.

D. Atomic bombs were dropped in Japan.

E. All of the above.

6

Which U.S. president was in charge during most of World War II?

A. Franklin Delano Roosevelt

B. William Howard Taft

C. Abraham Lincoln

D. George Washington

E. Theodore Roosevelt

7

How many victory gardens were there?

A. 7   C. 73,238

B. 187   D. 20 million

           E. 197 million

Your own vegetables all the year round . . .

if you

DIG FOR VICTORY NOW

In 1941, Forrest Mars invented M&M's exclusively for the military so soldiers could have transportable, heat-resistant chocolate.

The Sixties:
Flower Power, Apollo, and Space-Age Food

A BITE-SIZE history

"**T**he times they are a changin,'" sang Bob Dylan in 1964, a lyric that perfectly describes this transformational decade.

The 1960s were a time of questioning; a tumultuous decade that included another seemingly endless war, a short-lived but glamorous White House nicknamed "Camelot" (after King Arthur's castle), a missile crisis just off Florida's shores, a series of tragic, violent assassinations, and the landing of a man on the moon. More young people began to demand equality for all, and they also embraced four mop-topped English lads from Liverpool in a band named after a bug—can you guess who we're talking about?

The decade started with great promise in the United States, as the young and newly elected president, John F. Kennedy, declared this would be an era that would finally give rights to all. He challenged everyone to make the country better. "Ask not what your country can do for you," he said in his Inaugural Address, "ask what you can do for your country."

Another of President Kennedy's goals was to land a spacecraft on the moon by the end of the 1960s. "We choose to go to the moon in this decade and do the other things, not because they are easy, but because they are hard," he declared.

Things got very hard for 13 days beginning on October 16, 1962: American spy planes had discovered the Soviets were sending weapons and building nuclear-armed missile sites just 90 miles (145 km) from Florida on the island of Cuba. Since World War II, the United States had been engaged in a Cold War with the Soviets, which meant that the world's two superpowers were openly hostile toward each other without actually going to war. The tension focused on U.S. concerns that the Soviets were trying to spread communism throughout the world. Kennedy warned the American public on October 22 that he was sending the navy to Cuba and was prepared to use military force to stop the Soviets from using Cuba as a military base. The world was terrified the conflict would start a nuclear war. Soviet leader Nikita Khrushchev ended the standoff on October 28 by agreeing to remove the missiles in exchange for the U.S. not invading Cuba and withdrawing American missiles from Turkey. The Cuban Missile Crisis was the closest the Cold War got to turning into a full-scale nuclear war.

In 1963, the civil rights movement gained even more prominence when Dr. Martin Luther King, Jr., delivered his landmark "I Have a Dream" speech on the steps of the Lincoln Memorial in Washington, D.C., on August 28, 1963, in front of 250,000 people. In what is now one of American history's most famous speeches, he shared his hopes for freedom and equality for all races, religions, genders, and people. "I have a dream that my four little children will one day live in a nation where they will not be judged by the color of their skin but by the content of their character ..."

Only a few months later, on November 22, 1963, President Kennedy was assassinated while riding in a convertible with his wife and waving to adoring crowds in Dallas, Texas. Vice President Lyndon Johnson was sworn in as president on

RUSSIA
UNITED STATES
Washington, D.C.
Dallas
FLORIDA
CUBA
TURKEY
VIETNAM

Present-day boundaries are shown.

DR. MARTIN LUTHER KING, JR.

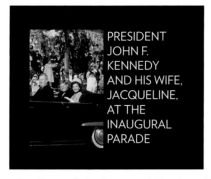

PRESIDENT JOHN F. KENNEDY AND HIS WIFE, JACQUELINE, AT THE INAUGURAL PARADE

Air Force One that afternoon with a blood-spattered Jacqueline Kennedy and the former president's body aboard. The decade's shocking violence would continue, as both King and President Kennedy's brother Robert F. Kennedy were assassinated in 1968.

Despite a shaken country, President Johnson tried to continue what Kennedy had started: He signed into law the Civil Rights Act of 1964, which banned racial segregation in schools and public places; the Voting Rights Act of 1965, which banned voter discrimination; and the Fair Housing Act of 1968, which banned discrimination in renting or selling a home.

In addition to all of that, a fierce war was taking place in Southeast Asia.

The United States had quietly been sending special advisers and military personnel to help noncommunist South Vietnam since the mid-1950s. The Viet Cong of North Vietnam were backed by the Soviets. On August 2, 1964, an attack on two U.S. Navy destroyers near North Vietnam was reported; five days later, Congress agreed to conduct military operations in Vietnam without officially declaring war. Thus began a nine-year involvement that would send more than half a million Americans to Vietnam and lead to the deaths of almost 58,000 U.S. soldiers. More than 300,000 came back wounded. Those who were lucky enough to make it home alive often faced anger from protesters who blamed the soldiers for fighting in an unjust war. The Vietnam War wouldn't end until 1975.

Despite all of the darkness of this decade, there were also major breakthroughs and achievements. John Glenn became the first American to orbit Earth in 1962. At the end of 1968, Apollo 8 became the world's first manned mission to the moon. And on July 20, 1969, Neil Armstrong and Buzz Aldrin walked on the moon. The entire world watched the black-and-white pictures live on television as Armstrong uttered what is now one of the most famous lines in world history: "That's one small step for man, one giant leap for mankind."

So did children eat a lot of Moon Pies back then? Read on to find out.

> " No one is born **a great cook**, one learns by doing. "
>
> Cookbook author Julia Child

A DAY in the Life: Bethel, New York, 1969

"Yum, orange powder." That's what some kids probably said in the morning, throwing a spoonful of Tang orange drink powder into a glass of water before grabbing a bowl of cereal, putting on a tie-dye shirt, bell-bottom jeans, and platform shoes, and heading out for the day.

Everyone would be talking about the big concert, the Woodstock Music and Art Fair, that had just happened in a nearby field and was attended by almost half a million people, or the outrageous white-wigged artist Andy Warhol (who once predicted everyone would be famous for 15 minutes) and his modern silkscreens of Campbell's Soup cans.

When they got home, children read the latest articles on astronauts in the newspaper and listened to a record by the Beatles. In the evening, they might have watched *The Ed Sullivan Show* or *I Dream of Jeannie* on TV.

At the end of the day, they would climb into bed and gaze out the window, thinking of how to make the world better in their own small way. They would do whatever they could, not because making a difference is easy, but because it is hard, as President Kennedy had once said.

AN AMERICAN SOLDIER IN VIETNAM

Astronaut John Young smuggled a corned beef sandwich into space on Gemini 3 in 1965.

THE BEATLES

Spicing Things Up!

Things were really a-changin' in the food world: The first shift was led by Julia Child, a six-foot-two-inch (188 cm) Californian with a passion for French food and for making it accessible and exciting. She, along with the French chef who headed the kitchen in the Kennedy White House and an enormous World's Fair that show-cased global food, led America to explore food beyond its borders.

On her popular public television show *The French Chef*, which began in 1963, Child inspired America not just to master the art of French cooking but to discover the joys of cooking at home and of sharing that joy with others. She always ended her show saying "Bon appétit," or enjoy your meal.

The 1964 World's Fair in New York introduced more than 50 million fairgoers to international flavors, from Korean to Belgian, inspiring many to experiment with global recipes in their own kitchens.

As foreign fare increased in popularity, so did two other food trends. Instant foods became huge—in part because of the craze for all things astronaut, like their freeze-dried foods, but also because of their convenience. Instant mashed potatoes, breakfast drinks, coffee, and puddings—to make any of them, just tear open a packet and go!

The other trend, vegetarianism, was quietly growing. Instead of meat, vegetables were the main part of the diet. Some hippies—a group of mostly young people who promoted peace—embraced vegetarianism and stopped eating meat.

JULIA CHILD

Table matters!

In the 1960s, manners and etiquette relaxed and more families began watching TV while they ate. Food manufacturers capitalized on that with frozen TV dinners. Invented in the 1950s, they were packaged and served in an aluminum tray and usually contained a meat entrée, two sides, and a dessert, all of which just needed heating up in the oven.

Common foods eaten in the **United States** at the time:

- Frozen dinners
- Frozen and canned fruits and veggies
- Frozen fish sticks
- Diet sodas
- Canned and frozen pastas
- Freeze-dried drinks, soups, and desserts
- Processed cheese and cold cuts
- Brown rice
- Veggies
- French classics such as boeuf bourguignon and coq au vin (beef and chicken stews)

Women at a Tupperware party wear the containers as hats.

THE SIXTIES

Kitchen Tools

CONVENIENCE WAS THE ORDER OF THE DAY, UNLESS PEOPLE WERE TRYING TO IMPRESS THEIR FRIENDS WITH A JULIA CHILD RECIPE. HERE ARE SOME OF THE CONVENIENT ITEMS USED IN THE KITCHEN:

Tupperware

These plastic food containers, invented in the late 1940s, weren't just useful for storage: They were a way for women, many of whom were stay-at-home moms, to make extra money by selling them at Tupperware parties in their homes.

Microwaves

Now smaller, these machines were used in some restaurants; there was even a restaurant in Sioux Falls, South Dakota, that advertised its "microwave cooking."

Aluminum Cans With Pull-Tops

Food and drinks could now easily be opened without removing bottle caps or using can openers.

Single-Serve Ketchup Packets

Condiments in mini packages made food more personalized and efficient. There was a growing obsession with drive-ins and drive-through fast-food chains, such as McDonald's.

MENUS OF THE
Rich & Famished

The wealthy tended to entertain in restaurants instead of their homes during this decade. The Forum of the Twelve Caesars restaurant in New York City offered two signature dishes: Wild Boar Marinated and Served on a Flaming Short Sword, as well as Great Mushrooms Stuffed With Snails, Gallic Cheese, and Walnuts, Glazed.

The rich also explored new "ethnic" restaurants, some of which had opened after the 1964 World's Fair, and spotted celebrities at cool hangouts like Maxwell's Plum on New York's Upper East Side.

YUCKY
HABITS
OF YORE

In the early 1960s, Jell-O dishes such as ring-around-the-tuna were popular. It involved a whole can of tuna, stuffed olives, celery, and onion all encased in wobbly lime Jell-O.

By the Numbers

65%: Amount of weekly income average American families spent on food.

$150 TO $300: Cost to feed an astronaut in space for one day.

Convenience and instant foods flooded the market in the 1960s. Here are just some:

- **Breakfast Foods:** Total Cereal, Lucky Charms, Frosted Mini-Wheats, Apple Jacks, Mrs. Butterworth's syrup, Pop-Tarts, Quaker Instant Oatmeal
- **Snacks & Convenience Foods:** Ruffles Potato Chips, Pringles, Yoplait yogurt, Cool Whip, Doritos, Starburst, frozen piecrusts
- **Dinner:** Domino's Pizza, SpaghettiOs, Campbell's Chunky Soup, Shake 'n Bake
- **Drinks:** Sprite, Coffee Mate, Diet-Rite Cola, Tab, Carnation Instant Breakfast Drink, Ocean Spray CranApple Fruit Juice, Gatorade, Diet Pepsi, Taster's Choice Instant Coffee

While in space in 1962, John Glenn ate his beef-and-vegetable and chicken-with-noodle dinners and applesauce from toothpaste-like tubes. Other "foods" he ate included veal and peaches.

Eat THIS

GROOVY EMPANADAS

The New York World's Fair in 1964 was exceptionally popular in large part because of the 110 restaurants that delighted people with international specialties. Originally from Spain, empanadas differ in every country where they're made, from Guatemala to Chile. While beef is a common filling, especially in Argentina and Brazil, we opted to make ours with chicken. You could also omit the chicken and do a rice and beans empanada. While the classic version uses homemade pie dough, we used a store-bought piecrust because we wanted to eat them as soon as possible! Serve with a crisp green salad.

Makes 20 Empanadas

1 tablespoon (15 ml) extra-virgin olive oil

2 skinless boneless chicken breasts, cut into small pieces

2 large carrots, peeled and diced

1 onion, peeled and diced

2 garlic cloves, peeled and minced

1 15-ounce (427-g) can black beans

1 cup (195 g) cooked brown rice

1/2 cup (100 g) diced tomatoes

1/2 teaspoon (1.1 g) paprika

Pinch salt and freshly ground pepper

1 box (15 ounces/425 g) 9-inch piecrusts (for a total of 2 unrolled piecrusts)

1 cup shredded cheese (the sharper flavor the better)

1 egg

1 Ask an adult to preheat the oven to 400°F/200°C. In a large heavy sauté pan, ask an adult to warm the olive oil over medium heat. Add the chicken and cook for 4 minutes. Add the carrots and onion and cook for 3 minutes more. Add the garlic, beans, rice, tomatoes, paprika, and salt and pepper and cook, stirring often, for about 6 minutes.

2 Unroll both piecrusts on large plates or a floured surface. With a 4-inch round cookie cutter, cut 10 rounds from each crust. Spoon 1/4 cup of the mixture over half of each round. Sprinkle with cheese and fold dough over filling. Using a fork's tines, seal the pastry. Place on a large nonstick baking sheet. Repeat with remaining ingredients.

3 Whisk 1 egg with 1 tablespoon water and brush over the sealed empanadas. Ask an adult to transfer to the oven and bake until golden brown, about 25 minutes. Ask an adult to remove from the oven and groovy, baby! Nosh on!

ASTRONAUT FRUITCAKE

This recipe is closely adapted from one that the U.S. Army Natick Laboratories created for astronauts in the mid-1960s.

"It was really fun making it with my mom!
Lexi, 12

Makes 8 Servings

Butter, for greasing pan

1 cup (120 g) all-purpose flour

1/2 cup (100 g) sugar

1/2 teaspoon (2.5 g) salt

1 cup (125 g) chopped shelled walnut halves

3/4 cup (130 g) dates, pitted and diced

2/3 cup (250 g) fresh pitted or thawed frozen cherries

6 eggs

2 teaspoons (10 ml) vanilla extract

Greek yogurt, for topping (optional)

1 Ask an adult to preheat the oven to 325°F/165°C. Grease an 8 x 4-1/4 inch (20 x 11 cm) loaf pan with butter. In a large mixing bowl, mix the flour, sugar, and salt.

2 In another bowl, combine the walnuts, dates, and cherries. Add the flour mixture to the fruit-and-nut mixture and stir until combined.

3 In a third bowl, beat the eggs well. Add the vanilla and stir until combined. Add to the fruit-flour mixture and mix until all ingredients are combined thoroughly. Pour the batter into the loaf pan and ask an adult to transfer it to the oven to bake for 1 hour 30 minutes or until firm and golden brown. Slice up and serve with Greek yogurt, if using. Eat up to feel like a space cadet!

POP CORNY quiz

1 What was served at The Forum of the Twelve Caesars?

A. Marinated Boar on a Flaming Sword
B. Flaming Boar on a Marinated Sword
C. A Sword With Marinated Sea Urchins
D. A Boar Holding a Sword
E. A Sword, Marinated and Flaming

2 How much did an astronaut's daily food cost?

A. Between $2 and $4
B. Between $35 and $36
C. Between $99 and $104
D. Between $150 and $300
E. Between $7,765,000 and $9,247,876

3 What did Neil Armstrong say when landing on the moon?

A. That's one small step for you, one giant leap for me.
B. That's one small step for a giraffe, one giant leap for an elephant.
C. That's one small step for my mom, one giant leap for my dad.
D. That's one small step for me, one giant leap for me.
E. That's one small step for man, one giant leap for mankind.

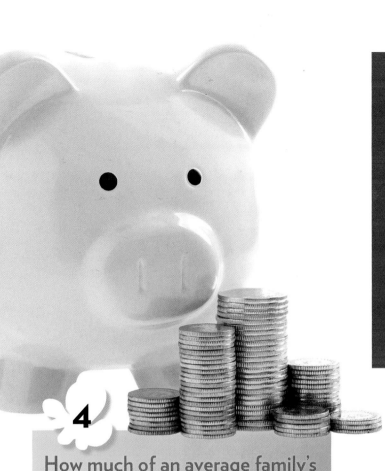

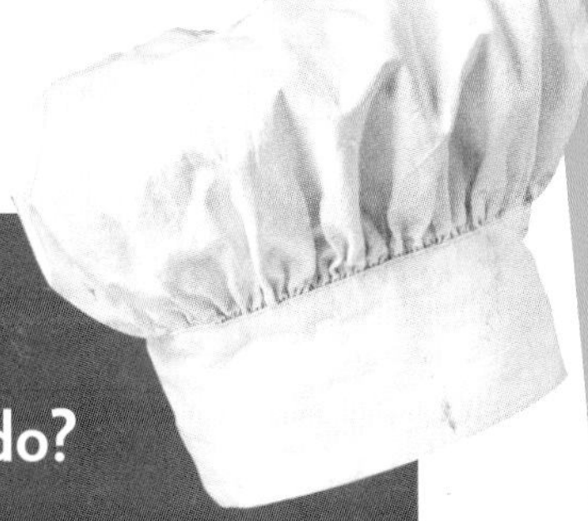

5

What did Julia Child do?

A. Made French food more popular
B. Made cooking more popular
C. Made the words "bon appétit" popular
D. Got people excited to try new foods
E. All of the above

4

How much of an average family's income was spent on food?

A. 2%
B. 3.67429%
C. 65%
D. 143%
E. 13,026%

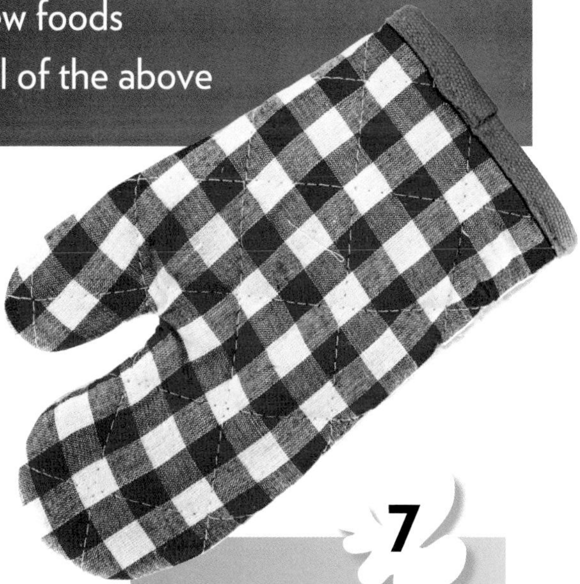

7

How many days did the Cuban Missile Crisis last?

A. 2
B. 6
C. 13
D. 34
E. 57

6

What was Dr. Martin Luther King, Jr.'s dream?

A. To have all races be equal
B. To have all religions be equal
C. To have all genders be equal
D. To have all people be equal
E. All of the above

Answers: 1. A; 2. D; 3. E; 4. C; 5. E; 6. E; 7. C

Future **World:**
Imagined Life on Mars

Space: the final frontier. There is almost no oxygen or gravity on Mars, it has crazy temperature swings (-195°F[-125°C] to 136°F[58°C]), the soil is toxic, and there's constant radiation. Yet by 2050, humans have figured out how to deal with those hostile conditions and have been living there for quite a few years. Life is fun, both for the Martians, as they like to call themselves, and those Earthlings, who number about nine billion. Let's get a glimpse of our future.

A DAY
in the Life:
Mars, 2050

"Ah, I'm sure toasty in my space bed!" That's what kids might say as they wake up at home on Mars. Even though the planet gets only 44 percent of the sunlight that Earth does, they sleep in solar-power-heated and cooled jammies, so no blanket needed.

For breakfast, they drink water extracted from the air and eat purple wafers that explode into different flavors and textures in their mouths: oatmeal with raisins and walnuts, followed by yogurt with strawberries and blueberries—all in just one wafer. It's filled with macro- and micronutrients as well as fiber, so nothing else is needed. While real food is still loved and eaten, "functional foods" (items that have been modified with added health benefits) in wafer, tablet, and powder form make a quick, convenient alternative.

Kids get dressed in pants and sweaters that have not only warming and cooling panels but also embedded computers. People can just look at their sleeves to read a story, check messages, or send a text. No more smartphones, laptops, or tablets required. Those are so 2018! And the clothes can change color. The wearer just says, "Green today, please"—and boom, green clothes! Or, since practically everything is created from 3-D printers, they can print up another outfit if they don't like what they have.

To get to school, kids head through their indoor apartment complexes—worlds unto themselves with parks, stores, and doctor's offices (which are the quietest places on Mars as disease and sickness are rare), all built beneath the planet's surface to protect the colony against harsh weather and radiation.

A 3-D PRINTER MAKING FAST FOOD

Children jump into the Hyperloop, which gets them to school in almost no time. Literally. While virtual learning is possible, everyone realized it's much more fun to actually go to school to see friends and teachers in real life.

Kids learn about the amazingly cool ideas perfected in the 21st century, from solar and wind power to how important it is to eat healthfully—for brain, body, and planet.

Students discuss how now that Earth is bursting with nine billion people, conservation is the order of the day: Solar and wind power provide electricity to large parts of the world; farmers grow produce on rooftops using hydroponics (growing plants without soil) and "meat" in labs from animal stem cells. Everyone is careful to limit water use and reduce the use of fossil fuels.

After school, some kids play soccer on a virtual soccer field or basketball with a virtual hoop, and then they head home. Mom sends a message that dinner is ready, and the family sits down to a real and delicious dinner of maple-glazed salmon with roasted broccoli and carrots and whole-grain rolls. The salmon is from a space aquaculture pond, the veggies were grown in Martian soil, and the rolls were squirted out of a 3-D printer before being baked. A robot could have made dinner, but the family did it because they love to cook together. They spend half an hour together eating and talking about the day.

At bedtime, the kids pull on their already toasty pajamas and snuggle into their space beds, thinking of the kids on Earth and knowing that they are happy and healthy. All is good with the universe.

PLANTS GROWING HYDROPONICALLY

Eat THIS

UP-IN-THE-CLOUDS BREAD

This is a gluten-free, cracker-like bread. To make it a fun breakfast item, you can add an egg yolk into the middle of the "cloud" once you let it cook for 10 minutes. Just take it out of the oven and make a hole in the center for the yolk, and then cook it for 10 minutes longer.

Makes About 20 Clouds

Butter, for greasing pan

3 eggs

3 tablespoons (42 g) cottage cheese

1 teaspoon (5 ml) honey

1/4 teaspoon (1 g) cream of tartar

1 Ask an adult to preheat the oven to 300°F/150°C. Break the eggs and separate the yolks into one large bowl and the egg whites into another. To the egg yolks, add the cottage cheese and honey and mix either by hand or with an electric mixer.

2 In the bowl with egg whites add the cream of tartar and beat on high speed until they are fluffy and form stiff peaks (like icing), about 1 minute.

3 Gently fold a little of the egg yolks into the egg whites, then gently fold the egg whites into the egg yolks until just mixed. Let rest for a few minutes.

4 Scoop the egg batter onto a nonstick greased baking pan, using an ice-cream scoop or a heaping tablespoon. Ask an adult to transfer the pan to the oven and bake for about 20 to 25 minutes or until light golden brown.

> " I must be dreaming right now! You bite right through it with no effort. It tastes so good; I can't describe it. "
> Tim, 11

POPCORNY quiz

 1 How many people will likely be on Earth in 2050?
A. 2 billion
B. 9 billion
C. 12 billion
D. 34 billion
E. 675 billion

Want to taste something stellar? Something out of sight? Unearthly good? You'll love these chocolate-dipped granola bars for their chewy goodness and their energy-inducing powers. Plus, they're perfect to wrap up for a pre-workout snack.

MARZ BARZ

Makes 16 Bars

3 cups (300 g) all-natural low-sugar granola

1/2 cup (50 grams) raisins

1/4 cup (35 grams) unsalted, shelled chopped almonds (optional)

1 cup (100 grams) corn squares cereal, crushed

1/2 cup (50 grams) high-fiber bran cereal

5 tablespoons (72 grams) unsalted butter, plus more for greasing

1/4 cup (42 grams) dark brown sugar (packed)

1/4 cup (56 ml) honey

1 teaspoon (5 grams) salt

2 egg whites

1 cup (175 grams) dark chocolate chips

1/4 cup plus 2 tablespoons (89 ml) milk or heavy cream

1 tablespoon (15 ml) vanilla extract

1 Ask an adult to preheat the oven to 325°F/165°C. Grease an 8-inch (20 cm) square or large baking pan with butter, line with parchment paper, letting some excess hang over the sides, then grease the paper with butter.

2 In a large bowl, combine the granola, raisins, almonds (if using), and corn and high-fiber cereals and mix well.

3 Combine the butter, brown sugar, honey, and salt in a 2-cup glass measuring cup; cover with plastic wrap and microwave for 1-1/2 minutes at full power. Remove the plastic carefully and stir until smooth.

4 Pour the butter mixture into the granola mixture. Stir until the dry ingredients are well coated. Add the egg whites and stir until thoroughly blended. Scrape the mixture into the prepared pan and press down with a spatula, a spoon, or your hands until it's flat and even. Ask an adult to transfer the pan to the oven and bake for about 25 minutes, or until set in the center.

5 Ask an adult to remove it from the oven and let cool until room temperature.

6 In a microwave-safe bowl or glass cup, combine the chocolate with the milk and vanilla and cover with plastic wrap. Microwave for 45 seconds. Stir well, then pour over the granola bars. Place in the refrigerator and chill for an hour or overnight. Cut into 16 squares and enjoy.

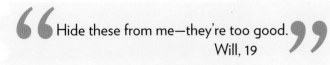

" Hide these from me—they're too good. "
Will, 19

" Don't hide them from me! "
Sanger, 19

 2 What is hydroponics?
A. Growing plants without soil
B. Growing pants without soil
C. Growing pains without soil
D. Growing plans without soil
E. Growing pans without soil

 3 What might the future's main mode of transportation be called?
A. The Hyperstoop
B. The Hyperloop
C. The Pooperloop
D. The Looperloop
E. The Looppoop

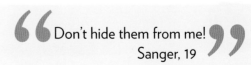

Answers: 1. B; 2. A; 3. B

Food TIMELINE

The epic Food Timeline created by Lynne Olver attempts to track the timing of discoveries of key foods, cultivation of crops, and the first known sightings of certain foods. New research continues to emerge, proving that some foods were being consumed by ancient people earlier than we once thought. Olver's research formed the baseline for our timeline below.

17,000 B.C.
emmer grain

10,000 B.C.
almonds
cherries
potatoes

8000 B.C.
wheat

7000 B.C.
pistachios
chili peppers
lard
pigs, goats & sheep

6500 B.C.
apples & crab apples
cattle domestication

6000 B.C.
spelt
maize & popcorn
dates
bananas

5000 B.C.
honey & chickpeas
cucumbers, squash & chayote
arugula, chicory & lettuce
buckwheat & quinoa
avocados & taro
milk, yogurt & sour cream

4000 B.C.
watermelons
oranges & citrons

3200 B.C.
chicken domestication
barley & cassava (manioc)
vinegar

3000 B.C.
butter & palm oil
peas & carrots
onions & garlic
apricots & spices

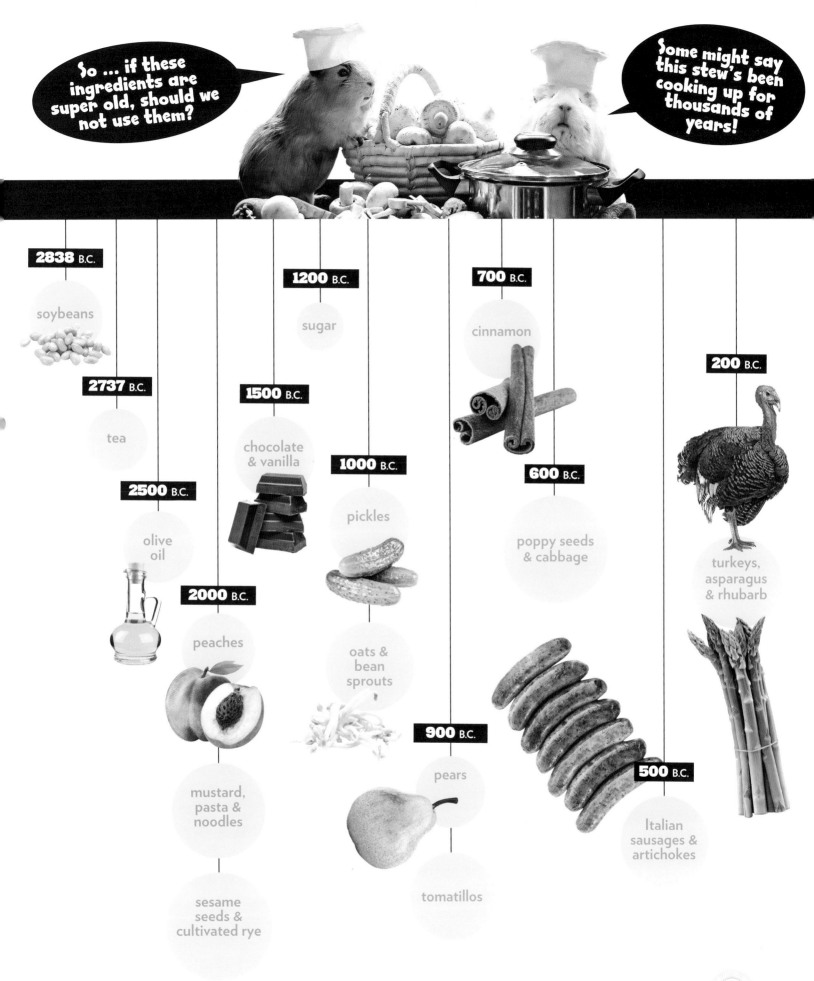

So ... if these ingredients are super old, should we not use them?

Some might say this stew's been cooking up for thousands of years!

2838 B.C.
soybeans

2737 B.C.
tea

2500 B.C.
olive oil

1500 B.C.
chocolate & vanilla

2000 B.C.
peaches

1200 B.C.
sugar

1000 B.C.
pickles

900 B.C.
pears

700 B.C.
cinnamon

600 B.C.
poppy seeds & cabbage

500 B.C.
Italian sausages & artichokes

200 B.C.
turkeys, asparagus & rhubarb

oats & bean sprouts

mustard, pasta & noodles

sesame seeds & cultivated rye

tomatillos

Acknowledgments

It takes a village to write a book like this, and I had the incredible luck to get the help of many exceptional people. Here are just a few of the many I'd like to say an enormous thanks to: my inspiring historian hubby for help all along the way; my beloved Wenman and Steel families, especially the brilliant two Davids in said families; my amazing friends; my incredible agents, David Black and Sarah Smith; my exceptional editors, Ariane Szu-Tu and Catherine Frank; and the wise and erudite food historian Andrew F. Smith, who helped me be as accurate as possible.

I'd also like to send a huge hug and gratitude to former First Lady Michelle Obama, who through her words and deeds always inspired me to reach for the stars. And I'd like to send a shout-out to our 280 Healthy Lunchtime Challenge & Kids' State Dinner families, with whom I will always have lasting bonds. And a special high five to those Challenge alums who tested the recipes in this book and gave of their opinions and palates, including Lahav Ardi, Aliana Arzola-Piñero, Will Bingham, Evie Braude, Tim Burke, Tess Boghossian, Sydney Brown, Andrew Chardack, Jacob Cook, Indiana Coyle, Abby Cornwell, Mena Choi, Kinnan Dowie, Hannah Foley, Miranda Gallagher, Lydia Finkbeiner, Orin Hayes, Michael Halpern, Nicholas Hornbostel, Lael Jefferson, Amber and Lexi Kelley, Campbell Kielb, Leo and Noah Koch, Ranger Lemaster, Roisin Liew, Esther Matheny, Jasmy Mavilla, Mary McFetridge, Charli McQuillan, Liberty Minson, Ava Nebben, Olivia Neely, Jack Newkirk, Owen Osborne, Claire Park, Laura Printon, Shakthi Ramachandran, Wyatt Rosengarten, Brynna Robert, Jacob Russell, Myka Smith-Jackson, Elena Sotobashi, Madeleine Steppel, Louis Teich, Hannah Torres, Izzy Washburn, Josh Weissenberger, and Braxton Young.

Bibliography

We used many books, articles, websites, textbooks, and cookbooks in our research, but there were a handful that were critical primary sources. We are indebted to these brilliant works and their excellent authors. We highly recommend you pick up a copy of their amazing books!

Books

Black, Maggie. *The Medieval Cookbook*. Thames & Hudson, 1996.

Dalby, Andrew, and Sally Grainger. *The Classical Cookbook*. Getty, 1996.

Erdoes, Richard. *A.D. 1000: Living on the Brink of Apocalypse*. Barnes & Noble Books, 1988.

Flandrin, Jean-Louis, Massimo Montanari, and Albert Sonnenfeld. *Food: A Culinary History From Antiquity to the Present*. Penguin, 2000.

Freedman, Paul H. *Food: The History of Taste*. University of California Press, 2007.

Kiple, Kenneth F., and Kriemhild Coneè Ornelas. *The Cambridge World History of Food*. Cambridge University Press, 2000.

Klemettilä, Hannele. *The Medieval Kitchen: A Social History With Recipes*. Reaktion Books, 2012.

Laudan, Rachel. *Cuisine and Empire: Cooking in World History*. University of California Press, 2013.

Root, Waverly, and Richard de Rochemont. *Eating in America: A History*. Ecco Press, 1976.

Smith, Andrew. *The Oxford Encyclopedia of Food and Drink in America*. Oxford University Press, 2012.

Spang, Rebecca L. *The Invention of the Restaurant: Paris and Modern Gastronomic Culture*. Harvard University Press, 2000.

Tannahill, Reay. *Food in History*. Three Rivers Press, 1988.

Toussaint-Samat, Maguelonne. *History of Food*. Blackwell Publishers, 1994.

Trager, James. *The Food Chronology: A Food Lover's Compendium of Events and Anecdotes, From Prehistory to the Present*. Owl Books, 1997.

Ziegelman, Jane, and Andrew Coe. *A Square Meal: A Culinary History of the Great Depression*. Harper, 2016.

Other Primary Sources

Archaeology magazine

BBC

National Public Radio

National Geographic magazine

Smithsonian magazine

Slate

The *New York Times*

Further Reading and Resources

Seaman, Tracey, and Tanya Wenman Steel. *Real Food for Healthy Kids: 200+ Easy, Wholesome Recipes*. HarperCollins, 2008.

Seaver, Barton. *National Geographic Kids Cookbook: A Year-Round Fun Food Adventure*. National Geographic Kids Books, 2014.

Becoming Human: becominghuman.org

Cookit!: cookit.e2bn.org/historycookbook

Food Fight!: kidfoodfight.com; natgeokids.com/FoodFight

Food Timeline: foodtimeline.org

Historic Cooking School: historiccookingschool.com

History for Kids: historyforkids.net

Kids Past: kidspast.com/world-history

National Geographic Kids: natgeokids.com

Index

Boldface indicates illustrations.

Text Copyright © 2018 Tanya Steel
Compilation Copyright © 2018 National Geographic Partners, LLC

Since 1888, the National Geographic Society has funded more than 12,000 research, exploration, and preservation projects around the world. The Society receives funds from National Geographic Partners, LLC, funded in part by your purchase. A portion of the proceeds from this book supports this vital work. To learn more, visit natgeo.com/info.

For more information, visit nationalgeographic.com, call 1-800-647-5463, or write to the following address:

National Geographic Partners
1145 17th Street N.W.
Washington, D.C. 20036-4688 U.S.A.

Visit us online at nationalgeographic.com/books

For librarians and teachers: ngchildrensbooks.org

More for kids from National Geographic: natgeokids.com

For information about special discounts for bulk purchases, please contact National Geographic Books Special Sales: specialsales@natgeo.com

For rights or permissions inquiries, please contact National Geographic Books Subsidiary Rights: bookrights@natgeo.com

Designed by Julide Dengel

National Geographic supports K–12 educators with ELA Common Core Resources. Visit natgeoed.org/commoncore for more information.

Hardcover ISBN: 978-1-4263-3162-6
Reinforced library binding ISBN: 978-1-4263-3163-3

The publisher would like to acknowledge everyone who helped make this book possible: Ariane Szu-Tu, editor; Catherine Frank, editor; Sarah J. Mock, senior photo editor; Dawn McFadin, design assistant; Mike McNey, cartographer; Molly Reid, production editor; and Gus Tello and Anne LeongSon, design production assistants.

Printed in Malaysia
18/IVM/1